GW00672036

Faces of Hachiko

Acknowledgements —

Published with the aid of a grant
from the New Zealand Literary Fund

The author would also like to express
gratitude to those friends who assisted
in the processing of the script.

Also by Ian Middleton

"Pet Shop" (Alister Taylor)

Faces of Hachiko

Ian Middleton

Printed and Published by:
INCA PRINT Box 540
AUCKLAND N.Z.

Distributors:
LINDON PUBLISHING Box 39-225
AUCKLAND WEST N.Z.

First published 1984

© Copyright Ian Middleton

ISBN 0-86470-011-3

Cover Illustration by Donna Hoyle
Cover Calligraphy by Kyoko Reid
Printed by Inca Print, Auckland
Bound by Trade Ruling & Binding Auckland
Typeset by Interset Type, Auckland

To my daughters Linda and Naomi

Part 1

Richard Mayne sat hunched over the typewriter, imploring the words to find their way to the page. The fan on top of the refrigerator whined through its incessant gyrations, spraying the room with blasts of hot air. He felt the weight of the ceiling pressing down on him, squeezing him. Distractedly he shook sweat from his face and said aloud, "Another Tokyo summer. I must be losing my mind."

Through the open window sunlight shimmered on the white flagstones in the courtyard that separated the twin apartment blocks. Beyond the courtyard in the car-park of the Rising Sun Plaza automobile bodies sparkled. Then the plaza itself rose, floor after floor of glass and pink concrete, filling a great chunk of hazy sky. Beneath it the yellow stucco blocks of Kimura Apartments sat facing each other across the courtyard like dollshouses at the foot of a mountain.

The keys tapped slowly, aimlessly. Please let the words begin to leap, the fresh white paper said, before the baby starts to cry and Michiko slams her door and yellow Camus comes to revenge his latest find on the iron staircase by my window. I have been waiting a long while, forever. Please let the words begin . . . .

The baby in the apartment upstairs awoke, crying

7

thinly. The mother, moving swiftly to tend the child, made the tatami squeak. Through the tenuous skin that separated them Mayne felt her moving, breathing. He tore the sheet of paper from the typewriter and tossed it into the waste basket. Then he stood up and began his mid-morning pace.

A figure moved brightly past the window. The doorbell rang. Mayne opened the door. A young woman in a red costume stood smiling at him. The smile was a mask for the fear and uncertainty in the eyes. How unfortunate for her, he thought. She was almost on the doorbell button when she saw, too late, the face of the foreigner through the window.

When the woman was satisfied Mayne understood her Japanese she told him she was selling economy priced condoms in luminous boxes of twelve. For the first time that day he almost smiled. No, he was sorry, he regretted he had no need for such things. It was indeed a hot day, was it not? The woman fled.

He moved through the kitchen, ignoring the typewriter, and passed between the sliding glass doors into the tatami room. The mats felt cool and smooth on his bare feet. The baby in the room above was no longer whimpering. He crossed the tatami and went to the doorway facing the alley. Between the grey alley wall and the door his mattress lay draped over a long bamboo pole. He reached out and touched the mattress, feeling the seeping wet patch. Anger surged quickly within him sending his voice harshly up the alley shaft to the apartment above. It was a bad matter to pour laundry water on someone's mattress, especially when it happened almost every day.

Turning back into the room he began to pace the tatami. The sun's radiance was burnishing the texture of the mats to a golden sheen. He looked down on the mats letting his tightness, his anger, be absorbed. Often, when the strictures of humidity and compressed living became too intense, he took off his clothes and lay down on the tatami. The tatami breathed. It was the closest he could get to lying on the earth.

As he moved back into the kitchen Mayne raised his

8

hand and touched the ceiling. How strange that when he had first taken the apartment he had been so blissfully unaware of the ceiling. A really tall foreigner would have knocked his head on it. Nor had he taken in the absurd inadequacy of the kitchen space or the dead-end world the windows let in.

Mayne sat down at the table and rolled a fresh sheet of paper into the typewriter. He was poised to hit the keys when the doorbell rang. He got up and turned the door handle. There was no-one outside. His heart began to pound as if it had switched to the core of his brain. The windows of the four apartments opposite and the flinting sky-borne eyes of the Rising Sun Plaza gave testimony to the presence of many people. But there was no movement, no sign of existence, no voice to call or answer, no comprehension. He shut the door, returned to the table and sat down.

Now he made no attempt to feed words into the typewriter. In a few moments, although he had anticipated it, the doorbell rang again startlingly loud. This time he sprang through the tatami room to the rear door. A little red shirt and dome of black hair was flying down the alley. "Come here," Mayne shouted, "quick." His voice rocketed through the alley, unnaturally loud, hoarse. Above him, while his heart continued to thump unbearably, he heard the sound of a woman's laughter.

The boy came to the stoop and looked up. The dark eyes shining from the round, unblemished face took in the awsome spectacle of the enraged foreigner. "If you do such a thing it's bad . . . terrible," Mayne shouted. But already he was beginning to feel the shock of over-reaction.

The boy looked up directly, fearlessly, into the towering face. "Please excuse me," he said. "I am sorry." He repeated this several times, then bowed low, the glossy black dome almost coming to rest on the great white feet. In a moment the little red shirt was moving down the alley, fluttering towards the ray of sunlight at the free end.

Mayne stood in the doorway breathing heavily, feeling the sweat sliding on his skin. He could feel the eyes of the

9

boy, so clear and unspoiled, boring up into him, could hear the echos of his own unreason thundering in the alley. Where rage had choked, guilt was beginning to flood. "What's happening inside this man," he muttered. "Another Tokyo summer? Never." He went back to the table and slumped down beside the typewriter.

Looking down into the clear ivory-limbed water Harumi thought, it's madness. Mother would be terribly angry if she ever found out. If . . . and she began to laugh softly to herself. But mother was safely at home in Fukushima and she, Harumi, was in Tokyo, drifting lazily in the piping heat of her Saturday morning bath.

Gazing dreamily into the water Harumi thought, I like my body, especially today. I like my rounded knees and thighs and the way my breasts tremble, uptilting on the surface of the water. The nipples peep out like tiny licks of pinky brown coral. In my bath there is no need of shame. She sat unmoving, tingling all over.

The face of Keiko from the coffee bar yesterday afternoon came to her, the eyes suspended in the dimness, clear, bright, alert, Keiko's hand reaching out, the warm fingers closing gently on hers. At last the cool voice beginning to chime with the ice-tinkling coffee cups: "Frankly speaking, Harumi, I think it's foolish for you to go to his apartment alone. You cannot know what to expect in such a place. I'm so afraid for you."

What was he like in reality. Harumi closed her eyes and tried to create him in her mind. But the telephone voice intruded, thrilling and terrifying her in the same instant. Her knees had gone weak. She had forgotten all the simple English phrases. How foolish she felt, recalling the stammering confusion in her voice. His tone, on the other hand, was so warm, so full of life. Yes, even if it was too absurd to pass on to Keiko, his voice had pierced her irrevocably. That was how she felt.

How old was he? How tall? What did he look like? She laughed again, a little uncertainly. He would probably be one of those round, jolly, red faced little men with white

10

hair sticking out of his ears. That would damp down her excitement and would not Keiko laugh when she heard of it.

She got up and stepped from the bath on to the tiny expanse of white tiles. Brushing the mist from the bathroom mirror she looked briefly into herself. Good, she thought, very good. There was a new expectant light in the eyes gazing back at her. The pink mouth and slightly flushed cheeks reflected the relaxing heat of the bath and the rise of her spirits. Even the strands of unruly damp hair that refused to conform to the will of her fingers and the flaring nostrils that usually irritated her were now reflected harmoniously.

In the cupboard in her bedroom Harumi found the green silk dress that she had been keeping for a special occasion and put it on. The feel of the silk sheathing her body and the tatami under her bare feet endorsed her well being. Did he like green? What colour were his eyes? You never knew what to expect with a foreigner.

By the little table in the scaled down living room she sat brushing her hair. Surrounded by her possessions, the colour television set, digital clock, chest of drawers with the family photos on top, and all the other trifles and treasures of the tiny nested space she felt comforted and secure. It was her ritual to rest for a while in the living room before facing the city. When she was ready at last she stood up, switched off the fan, picked up her handbag and went to the door.

Michiko opened her eyes and stared vaguely about the room, not yet daring to hope that she was free of the dream. She saw her clothes strewn on the tatami as if delivered by typhoon, and superimposed on this the hateful face of the gangster who had pursued her in her dream. The pock-marked, knife scarred cheeks, the shaven head, the hoarse pitiless voice. "Give me everything, everything you possess, or you'll be dead, be dead, be dead." The hand wrenching at her shoulder as she fled down the dark Shinjuku alley.

11

Involuntarily her hand went to her throat. She shivered. It was only a dream after all but it still lingered inside her. There was a terrible taste in her mouth and her throat was sore from too many cigarettes. What had happened in the White Bear bar last night? She remembered her first two clients, one young and shy, the other old and fumbling. Because she was at her wits' end with loneliness and boredom she had taken two or three strong whisky waters with them instead of her usual hostess's ration of coloured water. After that the night had melted into disjointed fragments of darkness and sound.

When, after alcohol, you lost touch with the world of reality, did not bad events follow? What terrible things had she done in those long lost hours at the White Bear? Since her last fall from grace, only a week or so ago, Akiko, the Moma-san, had been keeping a close eye on her. Consideration of what that all-seeing eye may have perceived last night terrified her. She closed her eyes and snuggled deeper into the protective heat of the bedclothes.

Something cool and smooth slid from her thighs and lodged uncomfortably between her buttocks. She put down a hand and discovered her vibrator. The switch was on. So she had done that as well in her blank moments last night. What next . . . .

How cold and lifeless the vibrator looked in daylight, so different from the way it felt when she was aroused and it aroused her. At first detachedly, then angrily, she flipped the switch, but the vibrator remained lifeless. "Another dead battery," she muttered, and every week she paid more and more for batteries whose lives seemed so much shorter. She tossed the vibrator across the room. It struck the paper doors of her cupboard and slid to the tatami.

Michiko got up shakily, put on a lounging kimono, and was heading for the bathroom when she heard the bell across the courtyard ring. She slid her opaque window open a crack and peeped through. A woman in red was standing by the foreigner's door speaking to him. "Ha," she said to herself, "the condom seller. Doesn't she know that her condoms are too small for donkey foreigners like him? Look at him standing there, smiling so cutely, the great white cream cake."

The more she saw of the English teacher the more she despised him, yet he always smiled at her as if he would like to be friendly. Why did his image fill her with such feelings? Was it the strangeness of his milk white skin, curly brown hair and grey-green eyes? After all, she had never seen a foreigner in the flesh until she came to Tokyo. Or was it just the sound of the word foreigner in her mind that heightened her contempt? Different, strange, foreign, foreigner . . . .

She shrugged, turned from the window and went to the bathroom. While the bath was filling and she waited until it was safe to light the gas burner, she tried again to piece the night together. Then she recalled with a start her sponsor Ishibashi was due to pay her a visit that afternoon. And Ishibashi, who was a member of the Shinjuku syndicate who owned the White Bear, was also a friend of Akiko, the Moma-san. Already she could hear Ishibashi's deep voice beginning to growl.

When the gas burner was safely alight she went to the kitchen and made herself a cup of coffee. She could not bear the thought of food, and anyway there would be a meal waiting for her at the White Bear when she arrived that evening. There would be time for her stomach to settle down. "Whisky," she thought, "whisky and men. I hate them both."

The foreigner's doorbell rang again. Michiko leapt to the window just in time to see a little red shirted boy from a neighbouring building scampering around the side of the foreigner's apartment toward the alley. She smiled to herself, full of admiration for the child, he so little and brave and Japanese, the other so alien and impure.

She watched as the foreigner opened his door, confronted the courtyard with puzzled eyes, then went inside again. A moment later she saw the little boy creep around the side of the foreigner's apartment and press the bell for the second time. Then the little legs were racing back toward the alley and she was saying from a heart bursting with joy and pride, "Go to it, little one, go to it." But her excitement was cut short by a sudden roar from the alley, a deep frightening sound, not human, more like the roaring of a bull. Of course it was the foreigner, she realised, it had to be. Only foreigners could make hideous noises like that. The sounds from the alley faded. She left the window and sat down at the kitchen table.

Sipping her coffee, Michiko felt the insidious stirrings of a melancholic mood. It was the awareness of so many people all around her yet no-one with whom she could pass the time of day. Even in the last days at her village, while she fretted like a moth for the glow of Tokyo, there had been people to talk to. It was true that all the eligible men had left for labouring jobs in Osaka and Tokyo. But the women and children had stayed behind and she knew them all like close members of her family. Time spent alone was rare. Wherever she went she was recognised. Here, in the heart of Tokyo with millions of people so close, she might just as well be a scarecrow in a rice field.

Two years in Tokyo. She almost wept at the thought of it. From childhood it was her dream to get away from the village and see with her own eyes the wonders of the great city. Tokyo Tower, Ginza, the fairyland magic of the underground. Memory forced a brief sardonic smile. The dream and the reality. It had taken her only a month or so to learn the stark reality of loneliness.In Tokyo she ceased to exist.

But, like the trains, the traffic, the seething streets, she had to keep moving. She could no longer afford to stand still. This was the city. You were the tick of its clock. If you stopped, its mechanism would mesh you into little pieces.

Michiko left the table, went to the sink bench and picked up a bag of food scraps. As she opened the door the sunlight hit her like lead between the eyes. She dumped the bag in the garbage can, scurried back to the shade of the apartment and slammed the door behind her. The shock waves, shaking the floor and walls, were gratifying. It was the only door she had ever controlled and she unlocked it with a key that jingled little bells, and shut it like a mighty slap on the face of the world.

14

Noguchi spun the handle, sending a continuous stream of shiny metal balls flicking and bouncing against the pins as they made their way down the face of the pachinko machine. As the lucky balls were gobbled up in the quick snapping, tulip mouthed goals, lights flashed and bonanza loads of balls tinkled in the metal tray at the base of the machine. The pachinko parlour was packed with players, elbow to elbow, and rump to rump in the narrow aisles. The air was hot, sweaty and smoke laden and the staccato clatter of the machines was deafening.

Standing with thumb fast-flicking and eyes riveted on the face of the machine Noguchi was a picture of spellbound attention. But if it were possible at that moment to penetrate the inner, fragile shell of Noguchi, to ask, "Where are you now, Noguchi, in that deepest secret space? Not in the pachinko parlour, I imagine," the answer would come, "No, I am climbing a mountain in the Southern Alps. Dark clouds have descended, obscuring the path, and I move slowly on upward into the darkness, feeling my way like a blind man."

Seeing nothing and hearing nothing Noguchi delved occasionally into the metal tray, transferring handfuls of winning balls to the little plastic tub beside him. With lightning speed he moved from image to image, plot to plot, sequence to sequence. When he plummeted to the realities of his daily existence it was through the reproachful eyes and soulful voice of his wife, Noriko. "It all began when you met Mayne, the English teacher. Ever since that day four years ago you have been a changed man. Do you remember, Koichi? I begged you not to go but you would not listen . . . ."

Four years. Was it that long? In the secret space Noguchi blushed and closed his eyes in reflection. For days the sweat of apprehension, and on the day itself the unheard of early morning whisky, then at last Mayne himself, not to be feared in a physical sense but so unspeakably foreign. In the early stages he recalled it was like being shut in with a benign but unpredictable being from another solar system. His hands shook like wind bells in a gale.

Gradually, in a strangled English with much recourse to the dictionary, the outflow of the inner self began. "I have, in English I think you call it, a literary mind. I see everything differently from my fellows. It seems I live always in the world of the outsider . . . ." Mayne had listened patiently, putting in a helpful word here and there. It is strange, Noguchi thought when the attention of the grey green eyes was elsewhere, but I feel I have some foreknowledge of him from another time and place.

When Mayne suggested he compile an English diary to aid his conversation studies Noguchi willingly agreed. Three times a week he brought the diary to the foreigner's apartment, where he read it, fumbling and laborious, on to tape. Mayne listened to the diary and corrected it and much of the lesson was taken up with a discussion of the diary and its content.

As the diary notes progressed Noguchi went deeper and deeper into himself, bringing into the light the milestones of his long and devious journey. From this probing another Noguchi began to take shape and an overview developed, bright and clear, ever gaining in potency. It was like looking at himself through a keyhole into a room ringed with spotlights.

The shiny balls spun, clicking and darting around the face of the machine. In the secret space, in a detached voice Noguchi said: I am like a stone on the bottom of a fast running stream. My life in my company and in my home makes no progress. There, life passes always above me, leaving me firmly anchored below.

The voice of his president broke in from the company golf outing at the country club the previous Saturday. "You go off, Noguchi, and enjoy the trees, shrubs and flowers while we golfers enjoy a round of golf." The smile in the president's eyes was so infectious that the company members gathered around began to grin too. It had become a regular part of their Saturday afternoon entertainment.

Saturday was now Noguchi's only lesson day with Mayne. The English diary was in his briefcase at his feet. He had translated some *tanka* poems he had written as a

16

child at primary school. While he was translating the poems it seemed he was actually back in the village experiencing the clarity of each long ago moment. He could feel the wind in his face, identify the character of the little houses. He could follow the line of the sea wall and could see his sister running along it in a red sweater, hair flying.

Noguchi transferred another bonanza of balls to the plastic tub. Soon his president and his colleagues would be meeting at the country club. There would be smiles of recognition and greeting and shared chuckles at the president's witty turn of phrase. On the golf course during the afternoon there would be much good humour. Later in the clubhouse faces would redden over whiskies and there would be a feast of laughter and comradeship. On a Saturday afternoon Noguchi was as absent from the minds of his colleagues and president as their wives and children were.

A stone on the bottom of a fast running stream, a Japanese businessman poet. Again his wife's voice intoned, "What is that you say? One day you will begin a wandering life in Japan? Where were you wandering with the foreigner last Saturday night when you spent seventy thousand yen from your salary? In Ginza I wonder?"

"No, in Gotanda. I wanted to show Mayne-sensei a typical Japanese bar on a Saturday night. He is interested in studying certain Japanese customs."

They were sitting on their haunches on the tatami facing each other across the table. Noguchi had been away from the house for twelve hours and was starving. He could smell the food already prepared in the kitchen. "Seventy thousand yen," she went on, "all gone, on bar hostesses and a foreigner."

All day between the demands of his position he had been wandering with Basho and on the outskirts of his childhood village. The telephone had rung countless times and twice he had been connected with his president. The union delegates had tramped in and out of his office full of new grievances, and trays of the newly designed plastic button had been placed on his desk for his approval. The factory hummed. Noguchi wandered on.

17

"I heard a woman in the market the other day say, 'All foreigners are cunning. They will cheat you.' Does your English teacher also teach you how to make your money disappear?"

"I have been gone from this house since early in the morning," Noguchi's voice snapped suddenly. "I am hungry. Please lay before me my dinner."

Like coming from a dream, Noguchi's eye beheld the red tulip mouths gobbling up the shiny balls. A cascade of tinkling sound was filling the tray at the base of his machine. Already the little plastic tub was almost overflowing.

Michiko rode high, thighs widespread, sweating, looking down on the face of her sponsor. His eyes stared fixedly up at the ceiling as if in mesmeric focus on some unmoving fly. Moisture sucked like wet kisses between her flesh and his. Through his open lips little grunts were slowly turning into larger grunts. "Iku, iku, iku, iku," she cooed softly, hoping the signals would quicken instantly into him. I am so hot, wet, tired, she thought. He goes on forever.

She drifted into thought of Akiko. In an hour or so at the White Bear Akiko's shrewd eyes would be searching her, the voice so sweet, so gentle, so soft. "Do you remember last night, Michiko, when you spilt the whisky coke in the lap of Watanabe, the real estate broker? Do you remember how you laughed and laughed until we thought you were going to start crying? Poor Watanabe. The whisky coke made him so uncomfortable down there." Later Watanabe insisted on deleting five thousand yen from his bill.

How absurd Ishibashi looked down there, his mouth open, grunting like a pig, the big belly rising like a fat fish coming from the water. Soon she would have to start making more noises for him or when it was all over he would feel cheated and would be mean to her. She leaned back, raising herself high, then came slowly down again. A groan wedged itself between the grunts.

"Oh," she murmured, "it goes too far. It is hurting,

18

hurting. Oh, it hurts so much." Her voice sounded strange in her ears. In fact she felt little except the sweat on her body and the warm emanations between her thighs. How long had it been? Ten, twenty minutes? Time stood still during lovemaking. Love? She gave a silent derisive laugh. She had seen that only on television and movie screens and in the pages of books and magazines. She looked down into Ishibashi's vacant, flabby face and nearly giggled aloud.

The foreigner's doorbell rang. Who was it this time to see the big white donkey. He would be standing in the doorway, smiling his charming smile as if the bulge in his jeans could not be seen by delicate civilised eyes. Donkey, she thought, great white donkey, and she felt the sudden unexpected bounty of Ishibashi quickening within her.

She bore down, riding harder and faster on the quivering hips and thighs. His grunts rose now like fits of deep unhappy laughter. "Iku, iku," she breathed softly, then "iku, iku, iku, iku, iku," until her voice lost control and she was panting and could not stop moving on him. At last she sank down on his chest, letting the tremors fade in the slow reflexive movement of her buttocks.

Harumi stood by the door, her finger on the button. At the bottom of the flight of steps leading to the courtyard she had paused and dabbed her wet face and neck with an ineffectual handkerchief. A teasing voice said: You are free, aren't you. Then run away into the sunlight and forget this unmet foreigner who makes your heart thud like the big drums of Obon. She pressed the bell.

A chair scraped. She kept her eyes on the door avoiding at all cost the square of open window. The door swung open and Richard Mayne was standing back on the edge of the shoe-changing alcove. She saw him through a mind full of delicately placed mirrors that allowed her to look at him obliquely without fear of meeting his eyes. She was trembling. Her mouth was as dry as pumice.

"You are Harumi," he said, smiling at her. "I have slippers for you. Please come in."

19

Without a word she shut the door, slipped off her shoes and put on the slippers waiting for her on the lino. How foolish, she thought. You practised the words a hundred times and now you blush and fumble like a self-conscious child on her first day at school. But my mouth, it's so dry. I will never be able to say a word.

Mayne guided her to a seat at the table and sat down opposite her. "You are punctual." He was smiling at her. "Right on time. I'm glad you could come. Just take your time and don't be anxious about anything. It's far too hot for that."

She could not quite smile but managed to whisper at last, "Yes, it's terribly hot." There was a wet patch on his dark red T-shirt. It fascinated her. It made him somehow less foreign, more human.

He handed her a card on which his name, address and telephone number were printed in English and Japanese. Harumi's eyes were at last beginning to rest on him. Beneath his smile and the unhurried flow of his words he was thinking: beautiful is inappropriate, superb is better, but perhaps unreal is closer. He was very conscious of the patch of cold sweat on his chest. "Now, shall we see how much English you have studied and how much has remained with you?"

While he checked her English level and took details of her education she began to experience the depths of his grey-green eyes. Each time the eyes met her they took her deeply into him. Strange, tingling spasms shivered up her spine. It was like a rare, psychic moment in a symphony concert or when a thought strikes suddenly just before sleep. But it's me, she thought, and it's real . . . .

Mayne said, " I suppose I'm the first foreigner you've ever met. Is it a very terrifying experience?" He laughed, his damp, dark brown hair looping over his forehead.

Harumi blushed and crossed her thighs tightly under the table. At that moment the eyes and the strange rich voice were almost overpowering. "Yes," she managed at last. "You are the first foreigner but I am not so afraid," and she smiled a little. The thought came bouncing in like a wave from a dark horizon. Miso meru. Love at first

20

sight. But like death, it came only to someone else. She felt a nauseous ache welling up in her throat.

"You didn't ask the name of my country. Can you guess where I am from?"

"You are an American, aren't you?" It did not occur to her that he could be of any other nationality. Americans were frank, easy going and generous. Everyone knew that, and he, who was about to become her teacher, was so gentle as well.

"No." Mayne was grinning, not at her but at the puzzled look dawning in her eyes. "I come from a little group of islands at the bottom of the world called New Zealand. I am a native speaker of English."

Harumi was disappointed. He had so handsomely filled the image of the American and now she had no familiar country by which she could identify him. "New Zealand," she murmured after a while. "I think it is Queen's English there."

Mayne fluttered his eyelashes, grinning at his own private joke. "To some it is known as Queen's English." He stressed the Queen. "But I think of it as just my language, my basic means of communication." The uncertainty in the dark, superbly clear eyes told him he had lost her. Never mind, the language they were to use together could not be wholly dependent on words.

"I think your country is very beautiful." In the depths of her mind she found faded television images of mountains, forests and lakes. She also recalled kiwifruit, mutton, and massive rugby football players all in black. But these images were too unclear to mention. "And I think you have a splendid mountain like Fuji. Egmont, I think."

"Yes, and it was a beautiful country until our great white forefathers got their hands on it. There was another language too but that's almost as dead now as the ash from the burnt-off native forests." Sweat was trickling down his body and gathering unbearably in the tight cupped fabric at his groin. Harumi sat straight, looking at him, unbelievably cool, her hands relaxed in her lap. "Why do you wish to study English conversation with

21

me?"

The unexpected change of direction startled her. In her confusion, the sounds coming from his lips were unrelated to language. At that moment the English teacher could have been a visitor from outer space. The question had to be repeated several times before she finally heard it. Then she heard her faltering voice saying, "One day I want to go away from Japan and visit foreign countries." Why did the smooth, clear path suddenly change and bring you to an impassable place. She looked down at the table, waiting for her confidence to return.

Mayne got up, went to the refrigerator and came back with a glass of peach juice. He waited while she sipped the juice then said, "In English we often change the subject unexpectedly. It takes time to become accustomed to our use of the language." He looked at her, detached from the sound of his voice. How many thousands of hours had he sat in the dollshouse room, switching himself off and on like a taperecorder. Faces came, open mouthed, eyes dull, blank walls for his words to bounce off while he longed for the hour to pass. Now time was rocketing like the Bullet Train.

Harumi was smiling. "Thank you for the delicious juice," she said. "I feel, aah, refreshed." She was hearing her friend Keiko's voice: "When you are close to them it makes you feel ill. It is the pungent, meaty smell of their bodies." Yet, in the tiny, humid space of the room there was no suggestion of such alien flesh. Keiko's face would be a comedy of disbelief when she told her.

In little more than an hour Michiko would have to put on her bar clothes and prepare for the night's work. The vague plans for the day, cleaning the apartment, washing clothes, shopping, must now be abandoned until tomorrow. She was tired and her mind was racing from thought to thought like clouds across a turbulent sky. In her hot moist hand it seemed a great distance away. Ishibashi was getting big again.

I was crazy to come here, she thought. There, it popped

22

out again like a surprise from a box. I was crazy to come to this place where I am always a stranger. Now he is becoming so enlarged and my hand is getting numb. Ishibashi, you are as unyielding as granite and there is no other side to you. You never speak kindly to me, only want, want, want, want.

The whisky waters they had shared, after lovemaking, had fired him but induced only a despondent nausea in her. Bright colours were what she needed, the stability of green forest ranges; yellow green rice, tall, waving, and the grey house sleeping under the hump of the hill.

Ishibashi said, "Quick, quick," calling her down. She lowered her head and took the offering into her mouth like a gnarled and bulbous horseradish. She cupped her hand underneath, squeezing a little. He liked that. Her grandmother's voice: "Learn what the man likes and give him that. Learn it well and do it well and he will be contented."

It invaded her mouth and throat, choking out thought. His hands were in her hair, holding her fast as he went deeper. The tempo of his grunting had quickened. It would not be long now. At this point she was expected to begin touching herself. Limply she put her hand out of sight between her thighs.

My mouth hurts, Michiko thought. The hairs tickle. Why does he take such an age. I will not have time to dress and arrange my hair properly, and Akiko will scold me for being unkempt as well as for the terrible things I did last night when drunk. Please hurry, big horseradish, please hurry.

At last the grunting cries and heaving belly signalled the climax deep in her throat. She took him effortlessly, without tasting, deep into herself until the spasms had subsided and he was slipping tiny and limp from her mouth. Two years ago when he had first thrust her head down and held her tightly against him with his fingers coiled in her hair she had known only nausea and shame. Then the hot, viscous pulses flooded her mouth and she was expelling him, discorging him silently with her tears into a hidden fold in the sheet. The taste of her shame

23

\eated her for days. There was no one she could tell. ..,ow she felt nothing but boredom. It was no more than taking noodles on the end of chopsticks and feeding them through drunken lips. She tasted nothing. Inside there was no longer any self-contempt. The heaving belly was still. She raised her head from the sweating pungent odour of his flesh. His eyes were shut. Soon he would begin to snore. She got quickly to her feet.

I wear a dark suit and I look like a businessman. But I am a poet. Can you hear me? Noguchi's eyes, growing accustomed to the half light, were increasing in range. The room was vast. He could not yet pick up the distant walls. He spoke with candid eyes to the centralised fountain which plumed in misty rainbow light and splashed its music on to a great marble bowl. To the Saturday-freed patrons, seated, settling and departing, he announced silently: I am Noguchi, poet. I have certain insights that set me apart, but do not be afraid.

He sat at a tiny, one-seat table, occasionally raising his iced whisky-water. The Steppenwolf paperback that had been in and out of his pocket for years lay beside his glass. On top of the paperback his two-way Japanese-English dictionary rested. In the briefcase on the floor, between his feet, there was a paper bag containing five cans of salmon, a gift for his English teacher from his winnings at the slot machine parlour. He checked his watch. There was an hour to kill before his appointment.

A girl in an elegant peacock-blue and white kimono rustled past Noguchi's table attended by a sleek young man in a black suit. They sat down at a table across the aisle from him and began a low, animated conversation. She had just come from her first calligraphy exhibition at Ueno and was excited by the response to her work. In the tight little spaces available when his enchantress paused for breath the young man nodded and smiled and repeated, "Well, honestly, really . . .?" Noguchi registered every word and added this new discourse to the many nearby conversations to which he was already attuned.

24

The flow of communication passed through him like an electric current, charging his mind, narrowing his eyes, causing a faint smile to stir now and then.

Without losing a glimmer of contact with the energies around him Noguchi opened Steppenwolf and began to crack the words open like ripe nuts. Every few moments he reached for the dictionary and gazed into it as if it were a crystal ball. Then his face would relax and he would say "Ha, ha," and "ah so" and the dark figure of Steppenwolf gliding along a street or sitting in a dim cafe would lighten. But the exploded words, no matter how hard he worked with the dictionary, would not let him into the more subtle byways of the narrative. This in no way deterred his efforts. All his life he had been moving through his own darkness. He glanced up from the book, letting his eyes draw in the suggested realities of his surroundings. Was not the transient uncertainty of the Funsui coffee lounge on a Saturday afternoon just one more timeless step on the path of Noguchi, poet and dreamer?

The waitress came, took his glass and his request for another drink and paused to wipe his table top. She was tall and slender and her scarlet covered abdomen was level with Noguchi's eyes. For a moment as she worked his breath fanned the inner side of her thighs. So close, he thought, and in the way of our people, so remote. Then the image of his president came to him, on the golf course, surrounded by admiring colleagues, about to swing his club. As the inner chuckle began the waitress moved swiftly away.

The fountain splashed like timeless music in a mountain stream. Noguchi sipped his fresh whisky-water. The peacock-blue and white kimono leaned ever closer to the young man in the black suit. Noguchi thought of his teacher's words the previous week. "To tell the truth, Noguchi, I don't think any human being could have experienced the changes you've known and end up in one piece." Am I one piece, Noguchi wondered. One piece of what, and he grinned to himself.

The humour faded. Questions. Since the earliest, haziest beginnings he had been set apart by and beset by questions. In the oddest, most inappropriate moments his mind had sprung the trigger and the questions had exploded like fire crackers in the astonished eyes of those around him. So long ago. The voice of Tanaka, the visiting dry goods merchant, thundering around the family dinner table, the eyes fixed like death sentences on Noguchi. The almost invisible father. "Send your daughter to, to university? Don't you know she might become a red?"

Little nine-year-old Noguchi the poet, round-mouthed, big-eyed, hearing the question sharp and clear as it flew from his lips and hung in the air: "What is a red?" The shock waves spreading and the eyes of the merchant oscillating in awsome disbelief, and his father's head bowing toward the table top as if in earnest silent prayer.

Not a breath from the kitchen where light years ago his mother and sister had been rattling dishes. Existence slowly suspending, then the eyes of the merchant somehow older, coming down. And the voice, trance-like almost in a whisper, "A red is a red." His father's face uplifting, the sound of his breath returning . . . .

It was at this time in the afternoon when the accumulated heat of the day and the massive weight of crowding buildings and unseen people bore down most unmercifully on the little room. If the time was free Mayne would strip off his clothes and stretch out on the tatami in the sleeping room. Then, one by one, he would switch off the sounds around him and begin the slow journey into darkness.

Now he sat under the whining arc of the fan as the conversation with Harumi began to weave its way to an end. An inner voice, becoming more insistent, said, "Tell her you are too busy, there are too many students waiting to join your classes." This, after all, was reasonably close to the truth, and she would at least on the surface appear to take the decision calmly. Then she would be able to return to the sunlight unscathed and he could go into the other room and take his rest on the tatami with only the bounty

26

of what might have existed between them. It was not yet too late.

But another voice, full of scorn, was stirring. Whatever happened to the heart that brought you this far, that beat without fear of the future? Take risks. Reach out. She is as eager for your spirit as you are for hers and she will not be put off by vague fears of tomorrow. It was in her eyes and you dared not believe what you saw the moment she entered the room.

Harumi was leaning forward, looking directly at him and speaking with more confidence. Her hands lay palms down on the table. What did her eyes tell him, she wondered. If they conveyed the merest glimpse of the sensations within her . . . she spoke slowly, glad that the practised phrases were at last becoming fluent. "If possible I would like to come for your lessons once a week in the evening."

Beneath the patch of sweat on his T-shirt Mayne felt the sudden upsurge of rebellion in his heart. It's too late now, he told himself, the decisions are all made. She is the clearest, most delightful image to enter this room. "Well . . . I am glad you wish to come. I'll be happy to teach you."

Throughout his teaching years in Japan Mayne had become so accustomed to the Japanese physique and way of thinking that it was only when he came unexpectedly on a white Caucasian that he realised there were other creeds and colours on the planet. There was no way he could see himself in contrast with the people of his daily life. He could not recall his own reflection or the approximate time of its dissolution. But the Japanese saw him first and always as a foreigner, as Harumi's eyes saw him now.

In his first faltering days in Tokyo there was little to distinguish in the massed faces of the city, no means of separating character and personality, just the anonymity of bright almond eyes and the sameness of olive skin and black hair. Seeing Harumi now, the smooth flawless complexion, the unwilting set of neck and shoulders, the superb clarity of the eyes, he was struck again by her

27

unreality. Put away the pedestal, he told himself. She is human, individual and frail as you are.

Harumi picked up the glass and put it down after barely touching it with her lips. His obvious discomfort troubled her. If only she could pour him a long, cool drink, make him laugh, ease the streaming sweat from his face. In some indistinct way she felt responsible for the heat and his condition. At the same moment she heard the scorn in Keiko's voice: "We have been the slaves of our men, those whose eyes are blind to us, for four thousand years and now you want to be the sweet little flower of a foreign man. Shame on you, Harumi." At thought of Keiko she almost blushed. But . . . that was it. He was the first man to see her. She existed and that was thrilling.

Mayne opened the appointment book and they began the search for convenient lesson times. The evenings were his busiest period and he was afraid she would select a schedule that would sandwich her between the lessons of other students. When at last, after much thought and consultation with her diary, she made her choice he was forced to suppress what would undoubtedly have been a broad and idiotic smile. The times she selected, all final appointments, were perfect. There would be no other students coughing and stammering at the door to bring the hour to a sudden end.

As he watched the pen moving in his hand and saw her name forming beside the appointed times Mayne was only vaguely aware of the baby's renewed cries above him and from across the courtyard a sound like the muffled grunting of a pig. He felt her eyes, curious and intent, reaching into him. She is thinking he has the lines of age on his face. But how old is he? His eyes and mouth especially his eyes, are young. And, oh, how uncomfortable he looks in this little sauna-bathroom. He felt her delicately wrinkling her nose, the thought slipping with satisfaction into its secret chamber. Not even the faintest whiff of anything foreign. Sweat, breath, flesh. Just the odour of the city. Japan.

He shut the appointment book. Noguchi would be coming soon and he felt the need of a breathing space before

28

his arrival. Harumi was already beginning to stir as if in response to the time signals of an invisible clock. He said, "I have learned so much in Japan. When you come to me I will try to tell you something of my language and culture. I look forward so much to our first lesson." Silently he cursed the inadequacy of words, the parrot-like phrases that were so remote from his feeling of the moment.

Harumi was gathering her things, smiling, standing. "This is my happy day," she murmured, and was stifled for words beyond that. In the moment before turning from him and going through the door she was afraid her body might lose its manners and do something out of control like touching him or jumping up and down out of sheer joy at being alive. She saw and heard nothing until her feet reached the steps at the end of the courtyard.

Noguchi mounted the steps and paused to mop his brow. His mind was baking like a desert. The thoughts he had been carefully processing for his hour with Mayne had been slipping from him all the way from the station. In his briefcase his diary and the cans of salmon for Mayne weighed heavily.

During the train ride from Shinjuku amid the press of damp bodies and obliquely probing eyes he had begun to think of the diary entombed in his briefcase. It was the diary of his inner, most private mind. On trains, in bars and while his wife and sons slept he followed the path of the pen as it laid bare his life and thought. Haphazardly through the eyes of the man, the child, the adolescent he saw himself revealed. As the pen began to work more and more industriously the entries appeared almost as the fictions of another self reborn.

On the train, with the briefcase between his feet, he had begun to think: that down there is my sub-soul; it is my creation and is not connected with my teacher, my president or my wife and sons. Do I strip off my clothes and expose my body to these crowding eyes? No. Rebellion and elation soared within him. My diary is the sub-soul of Noguchi, poet. It can no longer be seen by other eyes.

29

Noguchi was stuffing the handkerchief into his shirt pocket, picking up his briefcase. A mirage in green silk breasted the rim of the courtyard. The figure rose to gulliver height in the sunlight, then began to descend the steps. The eyes, gazing ahead, saw nothing until Noguchi began to move upward. Then they received him, alert and bright, with the clarity of instant awakening. They passed, close, she lively, heels clacking, he heavy footed on the steps. Ha, he thought, as he neared his teacher's door, a new student. Very very new indeed.

Mayne had just peeled his T-shirt off and tossed it on to the tatami when the doorbell rang. While Noguchi put on slippers and kept repeating how hot it was he got cans of beer from the refrigerator and set the full glasses down on the table. The after-image of Harumi was as bright as her physical presence 'had been. It was unthinkable that Noguchi should sink so wetly into the chair which had just embraced her. Poor Noguchi, so blissfully unaware of the great cosmic changes that had occurred during the past hour.

Trying not to look too closely into each other they touched glasses and said kampai. Mayne was conscious of the alabaster whiteness of his skin and the contrasting thatch of brown hair on his chest. "I saw your new student," Noguchi said. "She looks, ah, you taught me, a special case." For an instant his eyes met his teacher's, then he was lowering his head, sipping his beer.

"Yes, very special," Mayne said absently gazing through the window. Through the shimmering haze of the courtyard he saw Michiko's door and the dull eye of her tight shut window. Light danced and sparkled on the sea of cars in the carpark. The glare lifted his eyes, taking him storey by storey up the mass of the Rising Sun Plaza in search of the sky. At the fourteenth floor where the angle of his window cut the building's flight his eyes slid down again over the gleaming strips of glass. Nine, eight, seven, six, five, four . . . .

People, beds, toilets, stoves, colour television. Layer on identical layer stacked into the sky. Now the image of Harumi came between him and the plaza, following him

30

down to ground level, standing between him and Michiko's door. He shook his head. Drops of sweat ran down his shoulders. Noguchi clunked a heavy paper bag on to the table. He was smiling like a child. "I brought you a little gift of salmon. I was lucky at pachinko today."

"You are so kind," Mayne murmured, as Michiko's door opened, thrusting Ishibashi blinking into the sunlight. His stomach stretched his suit like a great black boulder, almost obscuring Michiko as she appeared in the doorway behind him jingling her keyring.

As if alone, Ishibashi strode heavily away, scowling at the world. Michiko turned to the door, slammed it and stabbed the key home. Mayne felt a sudden dart of insight and suppressed a smile. They've been making love, he thought, all afternoon and in that furnace, and now, all in the same breath, he feels flat as a pancake and mad as a hornet and must blame her. I wonder what she is feeling at this moment.

Michiko whirled, the hostile glance homing briefly through the window frame. Her head was high, her legs wide. The snowy whiteness of her blouse dazzled in the sunlight. Then she was moving swiftly past the window in pursuit of Ishibashi, bottom swinging, heels spanking the concrete. Noguchi said, "It's so hot. You taught me a word a long time ago. How do you say. Wety. Now I forget."

"Humid, sweaty," Mayne said, taking the fresh beer into his mouth. The space on the table where Noguchi usually put his diary was empty. "Did you bring the diary. I was hoping for more of your life, especially on a day when free conversation can become so difficult."

Noguchi's eyes dimmed as if there had been a sudden loss of power within. His lips tightened. A pulse in his temple had begun a tattoo. "I have finished my diary." The voice in his ears was strangely husky, rebellious.

Mayne picked up the lie. "I see. It has become too tiring for you to write your English diary. I am sorry that the window of your intimate life has now closed. But never mind . . . ."

"One moment." Noguchi had begun to fumble with his

31

dictionary. In a while he went on, "My diary is my sub-soul. Only I can look into it." He raised his head and looked into his teacher's face. Anger made his voice tremble. Even now my teacher knows too much about me.

Mayne rearranged his buttocks on the wet chair. Through Noguchi more than all the sights, smells and floods of words he had begun to know Japan. To him Noguchi was Japan. "Very well," he said at last, "from now we will just have free conversation. What time did you get up this morning?"

Through breakfast, the weather, the train ride to the plastic button factory, the conversation sweated on. Tension slowed the clock. As the unnatural, desultory words pumped out Mayne was seeing his friend, the little boy in the Kagoshima village. "I loved my mother but she was like a mountain half hidden in mist. I could not reach her. My father's eyes were blind to me. . . . ."

"I got back to my home at seven o'clock. My boys were studying in their room. I drank some sake before dinner. My wife had prepared rice, fish and some vegetables." It sounded flat, meaningless, like a lesson in Noguchi's primary school days. If only he could tell Mayne about the real world, the world of his mind and its journeys that day. Once, a long time ago, he had drilled a hole in the forefront of his skull and his teacher had fixed his eye to it. Now he must secure the inviolate insights of his poet's mind. "After dinner I talked for a while with my wife. Soon I went to bed."

Mayne banged down his glass, jarring Noguchi's eyes into full contact with him. "To hell with the weather and all the mad minds of Tokyo," he exclaimed. "Let's go to Shinjuku and get drunk."

Noguchi's smile unfolded, stubborn at first, then warm. "Ret's go," he said, accentuating the mispro-nounced word. Already he was bending, reaching for his briefcase.

Standing by the fountain in the square near Shibuya

32

station Harumi whispered dazedly to herself, "I feel drunk on sake and I don't care who can see." Her body felt light as air. The expectant voices around her and the splashing of the fountain entered her as melodiously as stereophonic music through headphones. She was tuned to conversations from many sources at once. Even the silent ones, and most waited in silence, communicated themselves to her. She had always loved the square, the meeting place around the fountain, and the adjacent statue of the dog Hachiko whose name had made the square famous. If you met anyone in Shibuya you met in front of Hachiko.

Whenever she stood in the square Harumi was touched by the legend of the dog, Hachiko. For years Hachiko had accompanied his master, a university professor, to Shibuya station and waited there for his return each day. In those days, the dog waiting at the square and dog and master walking in the streets to and from the station had become a daily ritual to the citizens of Shibuya. When death came to the professor one day Hachiko was waiting at the station as usual. He stayed by the station, day after day, pining for the professor until he too died. Everyone in Tokyo knew of Hachiko and the waiting place near his statue.

It was the movement in and around the square, seething, colourful, that fired Harumi's imagination. People scurried like ants at the underground entrance near the fountain and swarmed in and out of the tunnels and doorways at the base of the station building. They thronged in the glassed-in passageway that linked the station complex and passed above the boulevard at the other end of the square where all the traffic on earth seemed to have gathered for one last rally, people running, strolling, smiling, scowling, talking to themselves and by the statue of the dog waiting and watching.

On the near side of the square, in front of the police box, a truck bedecked with black uniformed young men was standing. Through a microphone one of the men on

33

the truck was pumping a noisy barrage of propaganda into the air. Under the square the rumble of trains agitated the earth. No-one near Harumi seemed conscious of sound or crowding. They could as easily have been standing on the seashore or in a temple garden. The focus of their existence was the point at which the awaited one would begin to take shape.

Near Harumi a girl in a red and white dress was casting quick alternate glances at the station and upward as if also in search of something there, into the pale sky. She was twisting the straps of her handbag and prancing on the same square metre of concrete like a horse on an idling merry-go-round. At last she gave a little shriek and clutched her breast. Then she was running toward the station. In a moment in a flurry of arms and legs she met the swift advance of her lover. They embraced fiercely, holding each other as if they hoped the friction of their bodies would unite them in one elemental flame. The last glimpse Harumi had of them was of two entwined figures undulating ecstatically toward the boulevard.

All the people in the crowd, Harumi knew, were not awaiting lovers and friends. There were students and older people from lonely four-mat rooms who came to the square just to feel the thrill of expectation in the air around them, isolating them from the blaring medley of crowd, witness the shock of recognition, the explosive joy of meeting. Then they would return to their tiny spaces and lie in the half light knowing that Hachiko was the closest they may ever get to loving.

Harumi looked anxiously toward the station. It was traditional for Keiko not to arrive on time, but to be twenty or thirty minutes late as she was now was rare. Possibilities crept into Harumi's mind. Sudden illness, an accident, a rejection based on some absurd misunderstanding? In her abdomen a pulse began to flutter. Near her a newly met couple were embracing one another. A hand touched her shoulder. She turned. Keiko was looking up into her eyes. "I took a taxi," she said. "There was a terrible traffic jam."

34

Keiko wore pale blue jeans and a primrose T-shirt. She was much shorter than Harumi and as round as her friend was slender. She looked young and vital, much younger than her actual years. Only the eyes looking into Harumi revealed her true maturity and purpose. While they engaged in a brief inspection of each other their clasping hands drew them close. Their intimacy created an aura around them, isolating them from the blaring medley of sounds and the eyes of the waiting crowd. Harumi said, "My throat is so dry. Let's go to Buttercup." Reluctantly they released each other and began to walk, fingers entwined, across the square.

Michiko watched the old Suntory running through the funnel into the Johnny Walker Black Label bottle and smiled sardonically to herself. When she first began to work in the bar and Akiko asked her to perform this task she was shocked. It is dishonest to trick people in this way, she told herself. In her village she had been raised on the old proverb that honesty is the best policy. She put down the empty Suntory bottle and reached inside her skirt to lessen the tight nylon constricting her tender crotch. Now she had learned to do whatever they, whoever they happened to be, wanted. Filling dummy Black Label bottles, drinking coloured water, letting the hands wander, what did it matter anyway. She had to work. She had to live.

She put the whisky on its shelf behind the bar, took a cloth and began to polish glasses. As she watched the cloth moving as in mid air the thought pricked unexpectedly into her mind. It had first come to her in a blank moment that afternoon as she was moving slowly on top of Ishibashi. Her village was disappearing. Its faces shapes and colours were misting over as if it were dying before her eyes. On first coming to Tokyo she could flick backward and forward over her past life at the village from about the age of three. In the early mornings when she returned weary from the bar she used to lie in bed and

35

rekindle her existence through the beacon light of the village.

How the gaps had widened in the milestones of her earlier life. The village was still there; the letters she received now and then from her grandmother were proof of that. And there were no more entreaties to return. These days the tired old hand simply inscribed the state of the weather, the nature of the vegetables in the garden near the old house and the wish that Michiko would take care of herself and not catch cold in that big city.

"Am I going mad?" she whispered to herself, turning from the mirror behind the bar. Nineteen years of festival seasons, gazing at the moon above the hills as it rose from the dark unknown world beyond the village, cherry blossom viewing, planting rice with her family, warming her hands inside her kimono sleeves on the first day of New Year. She shut her eyes. Blackness. In the darkest night of the old house she could reach out and recreate the village all around her. It extended from her like the limbs of her body. Now it was gone.

The foreigner inexplicably invaded her mind. She saw his pale face streaked with sweat, his technicolour eyes measuring her through the window. Why did he frustrate her so much, make her want to scream, bite and shout ugly words whenever she thought of him. Was it because he had lost his origin too? No. It was because he was a foreigner and only that. Cat's piss. . . . "Michiko, good evening." Akiko's voice came silkily from the other side of the bar.

If the cloth had not been stuffed so firmly inside the glass would have shattered on the floor. Akiko had materialised as silently as a cat. She stood smiling sweetly, wearing her western clothes like a fancy dress. She was tiny, a round faced Japanese doll. Above the smiling little mouth the eyes were set like chilled almond glass. She looked obscene in anything but a kimono. "Good evening," Michiko murmured, feeling the heat prickling in her face. "It is indeed hot, isn't it."

"It is so, indeed." Akiko placed her hands on the bar.

"I hope you are well this evening Michiko." She had stopped smiling. "No headache? There will be many customers tonight." She seemed on the verge of saying something further, then turned and moved silently away.

Michiko sighed and fixed her attention on the bar mirror. She ran the polishing cloth over its candid surface squeaking it vigorously across her tired eyes and broad face. Her throat felt dry. There was a part bottle of whisky under the bar but she dare not touch it. She felt the tender ache between her thighs and she thought of death. She smiled at the mirror, that now sparkled like diamonds, and put away the cloth.

The night passed in stages, at first calm with good-evening smiles. Then, as the liquor flowed and the noise level increased, decorum slowly vanished from the bar. The other three hostesses, also country girls, had not yet been sufficiently bruised by their trade to make their gaiety wholly synthetic. They laughed, remonstrated shrilly and slapped roving hands. Akiko had a steady stream of clients in her booth but busy as she was she seemed able to record every touch and transaction in the room.

Michiko's last client of the night was a middle-aged exporter named Ogawa. He had just returned from a business trip to the United States and was brimming with new-found knowledge of the ways of the foreigner. With practised chopsticks she steered some noodles between his lips then whiped his mouth with a damp face-cloth. While she waited for him to complete the mouthful she watched his face with the absorbed attention of a devoted mother. His hand was on the outside of her skirt, creeping slowly up her thigh.

Michiko was thinking even if Ogawa's clothes and voice were more refined than Ishibashi's how similar the two men were. In fact, after a certain point was reached, most of the clients in the bar looked and acted the same. It was like a well rehearsed game that was played night after night with only minor variations. If Ogawa's fingers,

37

moving less slowly now, were bold enough to reach the outer rim of her crotch that would be two thousand yen on the bill.

Ogawa waved aside a further mouthful of noodles. "Americans have their thoughts and feelings clearly printed on their faces," he said with indisputable authority. "We can understand whatever is in their minds just from looking at them."

When his fingers began to sense the texture of her pubic hair through her clothing and to fumble for the treasured place beneath Michiko did not mind. She sipped a blatant whisky, her third. Ogawa was a big spender. There would be at least forty thousand yen in the till when his bill was paid.

"Everywhere I went the American people were friendly to me," he continued. "We Japanese have an excellent reputation in the United States."

Michiko took his hand from her lap, squeezed it a little and placed it on her knee. She made no attempt to rearrange her rising skirt. On the next bold journey the hand would find its way inside her skirt. In her introduction to the White Bear the hands on her body had sickened her. She felt like cheap meat, chilled and dead where the fingers crept. She filled their glasses, raised Ogawa's glass to his lips and lit a cigarette for him. No, she didn't mind being touched any more. She didn't mind anything much anymore.

"Almost every night they took me out to their wonderful cafes and high class hotels. I have never eaten such quantities of good food before, especially steak, which only the Americans know how to cook." Ogawa's eyes brimmed with the potency of memory. "They were always smiling and patting me on the back. They called me Ken. I made so many good friends."

His theme made Michiko think of meat, mountains of meat. She suppressed a giggle. "What do they smell like?" She put her hand over her mouth but it was too late. It had just slipped out as from the voice of some slightly drunk rebel inside her.

38

"I beg your pardon," Ogawa said, elevating his massive stomach and staring at her. "Smell, what smell? I do not understand." His eyes were suddenly alert.

The room shook with laughter and squeals and the diffused sibilants of piped mood music. In the booth opposite little Mutsumi from Ibaraki was losing an heroic struggle to keep the big hand of her client on the outside of her panti-tights. Alternately laughing and scolding, with her skirt high up around her waist, she at last put her lips to the man's ear and turned her hips to him, obscuring his hand. The struggle ceased.

Ogawa's eyes were absorbed. He seemed to have lost track of Michiko's question. A little thickly he said, "In Chicago they took me to the Lions Club Headquarters. We had a wonderful time." His fingers had reached the outskirts of the desired place and were trying to find a way inside the nylon. "I even met a vice-president of General Dynamics. He shook my hand."

They came up from the underground passage they had been following since Shinjuku station into hazy sunlight near Isetan department store. The street they found themselves in was already drunk with anticipation of the night. They were carried in funereal slowness in a sea of people. The bright clothes and predominantly young faces said: let's say goodbye to our problems and the clock for a while and lose ourselves in the streets of Shinjuku.

Mayne, slow shuffling beside Noguchi, was thinking that he had never seen so many entwined lovers in his life before, not since he came to Shinjuku last anyway. The lovers, caught happily in the sea of flesh, were conscious only of each 'other. Heads close, arms around waists, daydreaming in their trance-like pace, they ebbed and flowed in thousands. If only it could be harnessed, Mayne thought, there would be enough massed energy among them to put Tokyo Tower on the moon. Love, he thought . . . the infinite power of love.

The image of Harumi struck him like a dart. Where

39

was she now. Sitting in some dim coffee bar in Shibuya with her friend perhaps, transforming her pent up thoughts into words. For a moment he shut his eyes, letting himself be carried along like a sleepwalker. In the screen of his darkness her face appeared instantly. She was half smiling, her eyes coming into him without reserve.

What is she saying to those expectant eyes, he wondered. The coffee bar is air conditioned, her skin is cooling. There has been enough time for her to take a breath and reflect on the image of the foreigner, now her teacher. What is she saying. Well, he's quite old and his skin is white as chalk. His apartment is like a matchbox. Even a Japanese would become claustrophobic in it. I got such a shock when I first saw him standing in the little room. There is a strange feeling about him . . . . Then the two heads closer together, giggling.

Mayne felt a new layer of heat creeping into his face. The lovers around him bumped rhythmically against his body, mindless of his presence. Some highschool kids floated past, their heads bent over paper bags. One of the group was laughing as if she were being tickled to death. Barkers cried from doorways and dealt out pamphlets like playing cards. Noguchi touched Mayne's arm. "Down here," he said. Then they were struggling through the street studded with bright paper lanterns, cafes and bars.

They came to a cafe with a red lantern and passed under a curtain into steaming heat and the shouted greetings of the solitary cook. They sat at benches at a long table. The wood was old, scrubbed almost white. While the cook worked at the counter, jointing chickens with incredible speed and preparing salads, his non-stop voice was in full contact with all parts of the room. With his tall white hat, fluttering hands and bright all-seeing eyes he was more like a magician than a preparer of food.

The waitress, young and friendly, brought glasses of iced water and hot wet cloths for their faces and hands. The tables were vibrant with easy-going conversation and end-of-week laughter. From the baseball game on the television set on the wall crowd noises broke intermittently like the crashing of waves and the roaring of the sea. Mayne felt the hot cloth draining the sweat from his face. The street outside was calm. The choking arteries of Shinjuku seemed now of another world.

The waitress brought pots of warm sake, green salads and grilled chicken livers on wooden skewers. Noguchi said, "Today's new student. What is her name?" He was pouring sake into the tiny ceramic cups. The map of Mayne's involvement had been clear to him as soon as he entered the apartment. There was danger. It was inevitable for them both. "She is a most beautiful young woman I think," he concluded.

Mayne drew the cloth slowly, unwillingly, from his face. "Her name is Harumi. Yes, perhaps she is beautiful, but we can see that kind of beauty every few metres in the street back there. I am concerned with the spirit inside, not the mask on the outside. I think you know what I mean." He was a little put out that Noguchi should perceive his feelings so quickly, almost before he himself could have known. "She is my English conversation student. If she is willing to learn I will teach her."

They raised the sake cups and said kampai. Then they turned their attention to the food, eating slowly and thoughtfully. There was time. At last Mayne said, "How is your wife these days? Is she still surprised that the terrible foreigner has not yet killed you?" And the laughter of their oldest standing joke broke the tension.

Noguchi grinned and shook his head slowly. "Every time a foreigner gets into trouble she brings me the paper and shows me. Foreigners are bad, she says, very bad, and she asks me when I am going to my next English lesson."

Mayne had to ask the question and hear the answer again, perhaps for the hundredth time: "Am I really the first dreaded barbarian you ever spoke with face to face?"

"Yes." Noguchi was reliving the shock and confusion as if seeing it all again on colour slides, the strange aura of the white face and grey-green eyes and the incredibly

41

foreign voice. He saw his own ivory hands on the table trembling like fronds in the wake of a typhoon. "Once during the occupation I said good morning to two American soldiers on a street in Kagoshima city. They did not seem to hear me. Another time, an Australian soldier came to our family home. He was the biggest man I ever saw. He had a rifle with a bayonet on it."

Mayne leaned forward. "You didn't tell me about this man before." Noguchi's eyes were remote, as if switching off a surge of inner pain. "And I don't recall it in your diary notes."

"Some things I can never write. They are just pictures in my mind." He was flushed by sake and the quickening interest in his teacher's eyes. These were only the shadows of incidents filed like documents within him, not the treasures of his sub-soul. "The soldier wore big muddy boots. He did not smile or say a word. He walked all over our tatami, disturbing everything, breaking dishes, walking on our beds. My sister hid in a cupboard."

Mayne tried to picture the obverse situation taking place in the sanctity of his family home, a Japanese soldier with rifle and bayonet and muddy boots tramping over the carpets, the beds, crunching the china on the dining room table, his sister hiding in a cupboard. From the television set on the wall sounds like crashing surf thundered from the baseball game. At a nearby table someone laughed deep and long. Noguchi had just reached out and refilled the sake cup. He raised his cup to Mayne. "To us," he said. "Can you believe we are both still alive?"

Buttercup was ablaze with jeans and shirts and dresses in every new shade and colour. Every available space was taken at the coffee bar and tables. The air was filled with sweet and spicy smells, the buzz of conversation and the overtones of non-stop pop music. Harumi and Keiko were sitting at a table sipping iced coffee from tall glasses. Keiko said. "I read in a women's magazine the other day

42

that life in Tokyo sometimes makes us so vague we don't know what is reality or fantasy any more." She looked intently into Harumi's eyes. "It is called urban neurosis, I think. Do you know what I mean?"

Harumi laughed softly. "Yes, and the women's magazines of Tokyo are just as mad as you think I am. They always have a sex story, you know the kind, that's so uninhibited that no good housewife should understand a word of it. And why do they advertise those vibrators and sex gadgets in such nice ladies' magazines?" She put back her head and gazed with exaggerated superiority at Keiko. "My new English teacher would say it's a — paradox."

"But how can I believe your . . . English teacher is as you say? I think you are dreaming Haru-chan. No man could be so kind and gentle and understanding, not even that Jesus Christ we hear so tediously mentioned at Christmas time these days."

Harumi was gazing absently into space. A phrase from a Japanese pop song had just shattered her consciousness. "Your eyes opened me like a flower . . . ." Yes, it was as if she had never been seen until that moment in her teacher's room. Sensations of his nearness stirred warmly. There was a catching nausea in her throat. She pushed her drink aside and cleared her head. "I never met any man like him anywhere. That's the truth Keiko."

Keiko sighed. "Then tell me about him again, but more slowly this time."

"At first it was his voice on the telephone. You will laugh. I was standing in the vestibule — you know where my telephone is." Poignant recollection made her pause for a moment. "Well . . . as soon as he began speaking I felt my body growing weak. My legs would not hold me. I leaned against the shoe cupboard, listening. My English words had all vanished."

"But what did he say that made you act like a little girl who had never heard a man's voice before?" Spontaneously Keiko laid her hand on Harumi's cheek as if to caress the truth from her. "I am anxious for you

43

Haru-chan, really."

"I have told you, it was not his words but his voice. It warmed me like the hands of a lover." Memory rekindled. She felt foolish, defiant. "But it happened to me. How can we ever expect anyone to understand our innermost feelings?"

"That's why I am so anxious." Keiko's tone was more gentle. "I don't want to sound like an old aunt but you are under the spell of a foreigner. It is the shock of his strangeness, the exotic side of him that makes your eyes look as if you've taken an overdose of something."

In the midst of a desire to retaliate with angry hurtful words the portrait of Harumi's mother suddenly suspended itself before her eyes. The eyes were wet with tears of farewell. The voice trembled a little. "You are alone now Harumi. You must take care. In Tokyo there are dangers for beautiful young women." To Keiko she said, "Why can't you understand? Richard Mayne is not foreign to me. He is simply a man, a member of the human race."

A group of highschool kids came in, their freed energies exploding like jumping fire crackers. They spoke in loud voices, the girls more strident than the boys, and behaved as if the space around them was entirely unoccupied. While seats were slowly found the noise of the group drowned other conversation. At last Keiko said, "How different they are out of uniform. In their classrooms they would be like frightened mice."

Harumi was trying to see herself and Richard Mayne in Buttercup together, the silence falling as they entered the room, the eyes looking nowhere in particular, watching every move. She is with a foreigner, an American, they are lovers, can't you see? If only her mother could see her nice obedient daughter now. See how he gobbles her up with his eyes . . . Harumi was thinking why is it always so terrible, so punishable when excitement stirs hotly in your body and brain, when you come alive suddenly like rising from the subway into bright sunlight. She said, "Why must I feel like a highschool girl when I talk to you of

44

Richard Mayne. If it was a Japanese man you would be so happy for me Keiko."

"If it was a Japanese man," Keiko's eyes were teasing, "I might even be a little jealous. Now, shall we take a little walk then go to my apartment? I really want you to hear my new records."

The sound of music and loud laughter crashed inside Michiko's head. She felt sweaty and half drunk, at the point where her attention became more and more focused on objects, letting her eyes loose in the object, fusing its reality to her mind. Now it was Ogawa's gold wrist watch, sliding up and down in the shadow of her thighs. It said 2.10.

It's strange, she thought. If I keep my eyes on the face of the watch the music fades and the laughter and loud voices die to a whisper. No, I am not drunk. The watch has stopped sliding now. There, its face is quite blank, like Akiko's face when a client asks for an extension of credit. Now the wrist is turning, the fingers struggling like fishermen with a nylon net.

Ogawa's tone was pompous, strictly confidential. "In the United States," he said, "there are no obstacles to a man who wants to get ahead. You just fit a picture in your mind then go out and get it — anything you want. That's the American way."

With the voice of an intrigued little girl Michiko said, "Is it big, I mean are the spaces vast over there?" She was widening her thighs, giving the last breath of encouragement to his fumbling fingers. "Can you walk in the street at rush hour without treading all over other people?"

Ogawa threw an arm around in an unsteady arc as if trying to throw a lasso. "Very big, very very wide. Most of New York is like walking in Ginza with only a quarter of the people in the streets. We can feel the freedom in the faces of the people passing by."

There was a sudden surge of energy as a finger passed

45

under the nylon. Michiko broadened her hips a little more. A touching fee was forming in her mind. Whatever it was it would need to be substantial and Ogawa could afford it. After all, he was now on the very threshold of that place. She raised his glass and waited while he slurped some whisky down. Then quite detachedly she heard the little girl voice say: "But what about pollution? I heard someone in here talking about Los Angeles the other night. They said . . . ."

"Pollution?" Narrow eyed, open mouthed, Ogawa's great broad face came to Michiko like a demon in the dark. "Pollution? There is no pollution, only the radical propaganda of the left." Beneath the nylon, as if beckoning to her inner spirit for reason, his index finger had begun an agitated waggling.

Michiko picked up her glass. She could no longer taste the whisky. It was more like gulping down hot perfumed air. I am not drunk, she told herself. The face of the wrist watch is clear, gleaming. It tells me the time has somehow jumped to 2.45. She turned. Akiko stood by the booth smiling. Beyond her, little Matsumi was sitting up straight in her booth, rearranging her clothes, fussing with the slipped-down necktie of her client. Akiko murmured sweetly, "We must finish. The police will be on their rounds soon."

Michiko excused herself, went to the cash desk and made up Ogawa's bill. When she showed him the bill he brought out a handful of banknotes without a murmur.

Before guiding him upstairs to the street she took him by the hand to the toilet. As she waited for him to come out, holding the steaming washcloth for his hands, the dying energies of the bar came to her as from a great distance. A shrill peal of laughter from Matsumi. The sound rising of Akiko's voice like a stranger in the bar, ripe and eloquent. The spaces are so wide and dark now, Michiko thought. I am surely getting drunk. Surely.

On the street she hailed a taxi. As the cab was pulling into the kerb she stood bowing and thanking Ogawa for his patronage. Then she was bundling him inside like a

46

large unruly parcel and listening for the correct signals as he gave his thick voiced instructions to the driver. In the wake of the taxi she stood for a moment in the street, breathing the odours of carbon monoxide, cabbage, putrefying fish and stale liquor. She looked up at the narrow band of sky above the street, searching for a light, a pin-point, a twinkle, anything beyond the earth on which she could get a bearing. But it was like trying to focus through closed lids in the dark of her room. She turned and clattered down the steps toward the bar hearing the precise beat of her shoes on the wood as if they were on the feet of another person unknown to her.

As she knelt behind Keiko, glancing in the mirror and bringing the brush down through the softly drying hair Harumi thought, she is so beautiful, satin smooth like a peach I could bury my lips in. Why must I see it now? She said, "It's a beautiful record. I love Vivaldi."

Keiko giggled. "Remember when we used to go to those terrible pop concerts. We thought we were adult but we must have been very immature in those days." She caught Harumi's eyes in the mirror and smiled.

"It was my first year in Tokyo, my first year at university. How can I ever forget it." How utterly charming Keiko is, she thought, without clothes. The shoulders soft and warm, the freed breasts uptilting, so large and saucy. They had taken off their clothes before bathing and it seemed even warmer now.

Keiko was kneeling, back straight, her haunches resting lightly on her ankles. Except for the mattress bed made up ready for sleeping, on the tatami, the room was bare. In the tiny middle room and kitchen beyond there were only the barest essentials of furniture. Keiko liked to move freely. Cluttered spaces annoyed her. She altered her position a little, relaxing her taut thighs. "Tonight," she said, "I feel a little vague, a little excited and a little angry with you."

Harumi lowered her eyes, absorbing the full ivory

47

sculpture in one glance. The body, in its own subtle language, had already conveyed its feelings to her. When she found Keiko's eyes in the mirror at last, she said, "Then tell me frankly, Keiko, why are you angry with me?" Underlying her calm tone another voice was crying: she wants me now, she's showing me, and I can't, can't .

Keiko's gaze was steady, almost nonchalant. "Oh, please keep the brush moving, Haru-chan. It feels so good. Now, why am I a little angry. Well . . . at last I can tell you. It's been on the tip of my tongue for months and I thought surely you must know my feeling but you gave no sign. I don't want to be like a sister to you anymore, Haruchan. I want to be your lover. There, now I can say it and the world has not come to an end."

The hairbrush stopped moving. Harumi lowered her head, her cheek almost on Keiko's shoulder. Through a curtain of hair she saw Keiko's eyes searching for her in the mirror and saw the lovely body displayed like a garden to explore, all the excitements of the senses in the shaded and overt places waiting for her. Slowly she began a downstroke with the brush and looked again into Keiko's face. "What can I say. It is a complete surprise to me. I am shocked." Where her flesh made contact with Keiko's she had begun to tingle alarmingly.

"Nonsense," murmured Keiko, not at all angrily. "Why, in this room only last week you were oh so ready, I could tell, and you pretended to fall asleep. And now the English teacher, the charming, gentle, frank man from New Zealand has intervened." Her voice had developed an edge.

"I knew this would come." Harumi tried to keep her voice calm. "But why were we unable to speak of it before? Now, at this time, it seems too strange . . . shocking to me." How many times had they lain in the dark together, holding each other tight and close, whispering the slow-ticking nights away. Always in Harumi's mind there was a possibility, more a vague dream, of something more intimate and erotic between them. But it went no further than her mind.

48

"Because we were too shy," Keiko said, happy to observe that the rediscovered eyes did not seem too shocked, "and because we are Japanese women conditioned not to reveal our deepest feelings. We were both so afraid to make the first move and we had to wait until one of us was almost at breaking point before it could be said. To live is surely to know the shame."

Harumi's hand trembled, making the brush strokes awkward now. The panorama of Keiko's beauty was so temptingly arranged for her wherever her eyes rested, no matter how fleetingly, she was captivated, the dimpled widening knees still pink and glowing from the bath, the hollow of her shoulder where her cheek had so often rested. "I know how you feel Keiko," she said. "Frankly speaking, there were times when I wanted you too, when I used to lie in the dark trembling inside, waiting for something to happen." It was the same tension she realised suddenly that she experienced with Richard Mayne, only with him there was no uncertainty. Something would happen. What would he think if he could see her in this situation. Would he despise her or would he simply laugh his deep foreign laugh?

Keiko wriggled her buttocks impatiently. "Men," she murmured. "I know that you are thinking of your English teacher. Can't you see, he only wishes to use you. At the bank our section chief has a book with all the women staff members' days in it so when we go to the company lodge on weekends our men don't have to waste time on lost causes. That's how men's minds work. Oh Haru-chan, away with men. Let's get drunk."

Keiko stood up and bent to kiss the top of Harumi's head. Harumi put her arms around Keiko's hips and drew the soft fragrance closer to her face. It was like looking into herself. The little black screen hid nothing. She moistened her lips. So close, so unbelievably ready. She could . . . the moment passed and Keiko was moving swiftly away toward the kitchen.

They lounged on cushions facing each other across the tatami, the tray of drinks between them. They were

49

laughing about their faces. It took only a taste of whisky to make their cheeks flush and now they were on their third. Keiko said at last, "But seriously, Haru-chan, why can't we be lovers as well as friends. The world is changing so rapidly it makes my head spin. Sometimes I feel I am flying through space. I need someone to love, to hold, to slow me down."

Already Harumi's head was becoming hazy. After the first drink she had been relaxed but now she was troubled by alternating moments of nausea, elation and drowsiness. Underlying this she was experiencing flashes of shimmering pale blue light and a recurring sense of instant communication with Richard Mayne. If she tried to explain this phenomenon to Keiko she would throw up her arms and say it was a manic delusion, the result of an obsessive emotional involvement with a conniving foreigner. When Keiko's face came at last into focus she said. "I know what you're saying, Keiko, but I am so drowsy I can't answer. I just want to go to bed."

Then Keiko was helping her to the bed and her head was pressed against the pillow and her hands were flattened on the mattress trying to prevent it, the apartment and the world, from flying free. In the remote darkness of her mind she was vaguely conscious of Keiko's voice whispering. But she could not apprehend the meaning of the words. Her last impression as her hands on the mattress relaxed and her eyes began to close was of a low cry and the sharp sucking in of breath as if someone nearby had made a wondrous and startling discovery.

Michiko left the taxi and walked on to the crunching gravel surface of the little park. There was just enough accumulated light from the encircling apartment buildings and houses to make out the ferro-concrete shapes of the prehistoric monsters who lived in the park. She found the lone bench under the silver birch tree and settled into it with a grateful sigh.

The park was only a short walk from her apartment. When she was really tired, hazy with liquor or feeling lost she stopped off at the park on the way home from the White Bear. On the bench, under its canopy of leaves, she sat in the dark, in the half forgotten night sense, feeling the clinging emanations of the bar dispersing from her flesh and clothing.

From the darkness of the street Michiko heard the sound of footsteps drawing closer. In the daytime, when the sounds of the city were blended, it was impossible to isolate anything. At home in the village her earliest memories were linked with the ringing of wooden clogs on hard earth. The far off sound of the clogs echoed now, the whack whack, whack whack rhythm of leather on asphalt. In the little park in the early morning, hearing the sound of other people only heightened her loneliness.

Two lovers entered the park and crunched over the gravel toward the seat. They walked awkwardly, heads together, talking softly, arms holding each other around the waist. When they discovered at the last moment the bench was occupied they turned away and went back to the street laughing and clutching each other. In their wake the odour of their union drifted to Michiko. Sweat, excitement, fear, sex, alcohol, tobacco — it was the odour of the city and it permeated her bar and her senses each night.

Where will they go now, Michiko wondered, to another park, a metre of sanctuary under some other tree? She had caught a glimpse of the woman's face, very young, upturned to the man, read the compliance in her soft voice, the need for quick repetition of intimacy with him. As the footsteps died away Michiko felt unaccustomed tears in her eyes. In her village, when mind and body yearned for it there was no man to touch her. In Tokyo, in the smoky dimness of the White Bear, she made her living from being touched. She had never experienced the carefree joy of strolling with a lover in public.

If there was somewhere she could go finally and shut the door, not the apartment but home, some place

51

familiar and loved that needed her, but the village and her grandmother were now as symbolic as ash and bone in her mind. This park, this night was the nearest now she would ever get to home.

Michiko shook her head angrily. Maudlin, drunk, she chided herself. Where is your spirit, your courage, your strength. You are alive and there are trees around you like brothers and sisters, birch, cherry, cedar and the night sense you knew as a child, and there the dinosaur, your night friend, stretched out like an ancient fantasy in the dark.

Yellow light splashed on the street. A taxi hummed slowly by. Not far away a car door slammed. Then a voice, thick and gruff and fluent with abuse, errupted in the night like a politician. Michiko left the park and ran along the street toward the sound. When she reached the bottom of the steps the taxi was pulling away and Ishibashi, still abusive, was stumbling on to the courtyard.

Michiko ran quickly past Ishibashi jingling her keyring and unlocked the door. As she dropped the keyring into her bag Ishibashi came up to her and stood swaying beside her. For a long moment he peered into her darkness, as if her face was some dim map or signpost to guide him on. Michiko reached past him and switched on the kitchen light. "Please," she murmured, "please come in." Her heart had begun to throb as if it was entering her brain. As Ishibashi moved ahead of her into the vestibule she found the door handle and slammed the night shut behind them.

Although no alcohol had been offered him for some time, every now and then with meticulous regularity Noguchi would say, "No, thank you very much, I have had plenty of wine thank you." To Noguchi everything that contained alcohol was wine. They were standing in the gut of Tarugoya, a small basement bar on the west side of Shinjuku. Mayne held fast to a pint bottle of beer above his head in much the same way as he clutched the overhead strap of a loop train in rush hour.

From the top of the stairs to the innermost wall the bar was breathlessly overcrowded. Mayne was growing weary. The boundless enthusiasm of the young people pressing around him and the space-age pop blast of the overhead speakers were beginning to spill over his tolerance level. It was like being in a train packed so tight that you knew there was no chance of getting off at your stop. There was no point in struggling, you simply gave yourself up to the bodies around you and stopped counting all the stations and miles you had been carried over. At some mindless point when the crush eased you knew eventually you would be let out.

Why the countless bars, theatres and places of entertainment, Mayne thought. Why not open up all the night free buildings in the city and pack the people in. Just standing together in thousands and millions, the known and the unknown, flesh fused to flesh, would be its own reward. "I love the rush hour trains," a bright-eyed girl student had declared a few days earlier. "There are so many people close to me. When the train jolts we all sway together as though we are sharing the same body. It feels so . . . how do you say, comfortable."

Mayne had lost track of the number of bars they had been in. All had been crowded and enlivened as the streets. As the night wore on he had also lost contact with his language and his past. In the dim milling spaces, supercharged with voice and music, he switched spontaneously from his native language to Japanese. The Japanese were not foreign to him and there were no white Caucasians to remind him of another way of life.

Noguchi said, "Yes, tonight I have had plenty of wine." He could feel the eyes of his people and the range of their speculation. The tighter the space the more spotlighted he and Richard Mayne became. How many people now in Tarugoya: two hundred? Three hundred? And Richard Mayne the only foreigner.

In the eye of the spotlight Noguchi felt himself growing

in stature. Now and then, in a low confidential tone, he was compelled to feed the speculation nearby.

"He is an international man," he would say to the eager eyes, "a true international man from New Zealand. He has been in Japan many years and has lived in other countries."

Now the eyes were enthralled, the drinking hands still. "The other day I met him at Hachiko, in front of Shibuya station. He was standing like a Japanese, looking like a Japanese. I said to him, my eyes see a foreign face, my mind sees a Japanese.

"Yes, he is a true international man," Noguchi concluded proudly, "and he loves Japan and what he calls the gentle way."

At times, as the attention focused on him more intently, Noguchi himself began to feel foreign, not to be compared with the alienation of the outsider but with the exotic appeal of the person in the public eye — the poet, musician or philosopher. At such moments Noguchi thought, if only my president and colleagues could see me now, they would not be able to believe their eyes. His family apart, he had never been able to speak to anyone of his relationship with Mayne.

Then, inexplicably, Noguchi began to think of his wife. He shot a glance at his watch. She would be waiting up, nodding off from time to time, saving it all up for him as if he had been a lover. After Shinjuku, his home was like a prison.

"One of these nights," Mayne said, "when she knows you've been out with me your wife is going to kill you, that is, unless some terrible barbarian does it first." He watched the smile in the attentive face turning to quick laughter. "Shall we go?" Noguchi was already bending and fumbling among the forest of legs for his briefcase.

The streets ran like tidal creeks now, all flowing to Shinjuku station. Waseda University had won a big baseball game that day and its black uniform ruled the pavements like an army of occupation. Drunk students and salary men sang haphazard songs. Lovers quickened

54

their pace as the gaps between couples widened. In the shadow pools of sidestreets and alleys men pissed like tottering fountains. Barkers in over-bright doorways, weary from the night's persuasions, stood croaking and smiling like clowns.

In a little square near Shinjuku station they came across two squads of Waseda students snake dancing and chanting their victory song. From one squad four men detached themselves and came quickly to Mayne. "Can you fly?" they said pleasantly, and without waiting for an answer they grabbed his arms and legs and tossed him through the air to the shoulders of the other squad. A crowd quickly gathered, swallowing Noguchi's unsteady cries of protest.

From the first squad Mayne flew even higher, coming down at last in the outstretched arms of the second group. Then back and forth higher and higher they tossed him. The sky dipped and spun with ribbons of blazing light. Free of the earth Mayne's mind soared and dived. He caught a glimmer of pale orange stars swimming in black vapour, a sea of upturned ivory moons, a jungle of neon squares tangling their blue and yellow light in the sky. I am going, going . . . wheee . . . almost gone.

From the shelter of the crowd Noguchi watched fearfully. Any moment his friend, his teacher, would be damaged. But how far and high they tossed him, the Waseda students, and how precise and sturdy their movements. A thousand questions were running through the crowd. Is the foreigner perhaps a captured CIA agent? Who is he, where is he from, what is he doing in Japan? How high he flies.

Noguchi was bursting with information. In the old days when a stranger entered his village and asked the way to a house, many people would gather. Much advice would be given on the best path to take and a child would be despatched to guide the stranger. Now Noguchi wished to stand before this crowd and teach them the way to the foreigner, his friend. "Excuse me," he said to two young lovers almost under his nose, "that man in the sky is my friend. He is a true international man from New Zealand." But the couple just kept staring upward, their eyes following in quick fascination the dizzying flight of the foreigner through the air.

Mayne's head came down hard on an unexpected shoulder. He was lifted, tilted, lowered gently to his feet. Noguchi came weaving from the crowd and took his arm. They moved through the skein of curious eyes and simmering speculation into one of the busier streets leading into the station. The night was emptying out. There was little more to say. They walked arm in arm, their bodies touching carelessly like two tired old lovers. Mayne touched the bruise rising on his temple. It had been a long long day.

A glittering ribbon of empty taxis slowly passed, the drivers seemingly unaware of the frenzy of signals they aroused. Noguchi was alternately signalling and muttering his irritation. When an owner-driver pulled up letting the door swing open they got in gratefully. Noguchi gave directions. Because it was easy to find, it was agreed that Mayne should be dropped off at the Rising Sun Plaza. He often found his way home from there.

Noguchi let his head sink back on the plastic seat cover. He was thinking of his wife waiting for him at home. No matter how quietly he tried to slip inside, she would apprehend him. One day he would simply decide not to go home at all. The image of Basho came to his mind and he thought of distant places, the Southern Alps of Nagano and his boyhood village in Kagoshima. One day . . . .

The taxi moved smoothly through the early morning streets. The dull throbbing in Mayne's temple stressed the anticlimax in the wake of Shinjuku. After Shinjuku on a Saturday night everything was an anticlimax, but unbelievably the day had also invoked Harumi. He touched his forehead, stirring instant ripples of pain. There would be long gaps in the night but she would remain bright and clear in the morning.

The taxi was coming to a stop outside the Rising Sun

56

Plaza. As the door opened and Mayne's feet reached the sidewalk Noguchi said, "I have had a most happy time tonight. Thank you very much. Are you O.K.?"

"Fine," said Mayne, wig-wagging an arm. "See you next week."

As the taxi gained speed Noguchi looked back through the rear window. In the glow of the plaza night lights he could see Mayne striding along the street like a vigorous sober man with a destination in view, only he was heading in the opposite direction from where his apartment lay. Noguchi was too weary to order the taxi around and set his friend on the right course.

Noguchi settled his head back on the seat cover. On the threshold of sleep he suddenly recalled the image of Mayne's new student and the new light in his teacher's eyes. Also, he remembered, on the train that afternoon a raven had come fleetingly into his window of sky. It was an ancient omen of danger. His eyes were closing. I have had plenty of wine today, plenty of wine.

Part 2

Although she had put it aside some time earlier, Harumi still carried the two pages of her mother's letter clearly in her mind. It was with her during her drawn out reflections in the bath and stretched out with her on the bed. While the sun burned through the apartment's thin concrete walls she felt her mother's eyes chiding through the pages. Lying on your bed while the sun is shining, Harumi, how is your life to be lived?

She felt slightly hung over and very restless. The theme of her mother's letters, always the same apart from the weather, never failed to disturb her. "Time is passing, Harumi, and you give no answer when I make mention of the future. It is unthinkable that you should continue your spinsterhood in Tokyo much longer. Each day I grow more anxious as I think of you so far away and alone."

She had been nurtured in her mother's womb. Her own maturity as a woman had made her doubly conscious of the eternal debt of gratitude to her mother for yielding her existence. When she was five Harumi's father had died, leaving her with no clear memory of him. The years that followed until early adolescence had bonded her closely to her mother. Then, almost overnight, it was as if their common language had been mystically replaced by some alien, incomprehensible tongue. The two-page letters were a consistent saddening reminder of this.

On a free, sun-filled day, to be troubled by her mother's letters was ridiculous. But then there was no way of predicting the acts and feelings that made you alternately bright and dull. At times, it seemed, two birds, one white, one black, flew like clockwork in and out of her window. The black bird was heavy with foreboding; the white bird bore tidings of peace and love. As one bird flew out the other flew in. There was barely time to catch your breath.

The incongruous images of her mother and Richard Mayne sprang up in her mind, she saying coolly to her mother: this is my English teacher, Richard Mayne; soon he will become my love teacher as well; already we are lovers in spirit. Her mother's lips tightening, the shock freezing her eyes. A foreigner? What do you say, a . . . New Zealander? It was as if the great Kanto earthquake was about to strike for the second time.

Thinking about troublesome matters only made the heat less tolerable. She wished she had found an apartment with more windows and a balcony, but she was so eager to live alone she had little thought of the long term needs of comfort and season. She got up, took the electric fan from the middle room and set it in motion on the tatami beside the bed. Just to breath in Tokyo in August was troublesome without the tedious words from her mother as well.

She loosened the sash of her sleeping robe and lay back. Fragments of last night's dreams began to coalesce. The dreams were so startlingly erotic and very real. She was lying on her back, soft lips were kissing her mouth, woman's lips. She tried to pull her face away; the lips only clung more fiercely. Deep within her an ache was growing, a wanting, hurting, physical, devouring ache. It was as real as the onset of the act of love itself. A tongue, small and wet, was slowly invading her mouth. She opened, her head spinning, giving way, letting it in.

Sudden pain ran through the nipple and aureole of her left breast. Her mouth gasped open, letting the tongue further in. Then, and in the dream, she was strangely without shame; she was sucking the tongue, all she could reach.

She opened the robe and arranged herself more relaxedly on the bed. She could hear the faint cries of children playing in the alley at the foot of the apartment building, the tortured grinding of steel on the railroad tracks and the thump thump, thump thump of someone doing exercises on the tatami next door. Surely they were real, they felt real, the hot cheeks snuggling at her thighs. She could feel them now.

Then the dream had begun to disintegrate. It was so hot and frantic her whole body was moving. Just before waking from the climax of the dream she had the impression of someone gasping her name. Then she was awake and Keiko's arms were around her and Keiko's lips were kissing her gently to sleep once more. In that tangent she remembered thinking vaguely that Keiko must have been weeping because her cheeks were wet.

Harumi felt flushed, almost suffocated with heat and memory. She took off her robe and threw it on to the tatami. She linked her hands behind her head and spread her legs wide. If her mother walked in the door now and caught her in this position, what a shock she would get ....
Daughters do not flaunt themselves in public or in the mind . . . . Irksome words from the letter infiltrated Harumi's thoughts. "Last night your uncle Hiroshi and I had a long chat. He was very disappointed when I told him that you had not yet registered at that marriage agency in Ginza. You know well, Harumi, there are so many young men of our class who have registered at such agencies . . . .

The telephone rang. She went quickly to the shoe cupboard in the vestibule and picked up the handpiece. The deep exotic voice, it seemed, was penetrating her even before it vibrated through the telephone. "This is Richard Mayne. I have a moment or two before my friend Kato comes to visit me. I just wanted to hear your voice."

Harumi clutched the handpiece tightly and leaned back

against the cupboard. Her legs felt like columns of warm water. If only her tongue would come to life.

"Hello," she murmured at last. "I was just resting. How are you today?" She shut her eyes, trying to erase the distance between them. He would be standing by his shoe cupboard, half smiling, her voice coming scratchily to him like a record with a faulty needle. When she opened her eyes she saw her hand covering her left breast. The nipple was still tender from the dream.

"Well, I'm not exactly sure how I am. I went to Shinjuku last night with my friend Noguchi. I think you passed him near my apartment yesterday. I don't know how I got home and I'm not sure where it came from but I've got a bruise the size of a goose's egg on my forehead . . . ."

It took a while to piece the symbols together, bruise, forehead, goose's egg, to make the picture clear in her mind. Then feeling came to her aid, levelling her voice out. "Oh I'm so sorry. I hope you're not severely hurt. Please, you must be careful in Shinjuku."

The quality of concern elicited a quick grateful laugh in him. "It's not too bad. I'm alive and talking to you. That's important."

Harumi felt the angle of the shoe cupboard pressing into her. It's foolish, she thought, childish, but I can't move. Only a romantic schoolgirl would imagine that a man could make love to you with his voice. At random she said, "I look forward to seeing you tomorrow, my first lesson."

"Until tomorrow then, goodbye Harumi."

Dreamily she left the telephone and went back to her bed and lay down. The strident whistles of passing express trains were drowning the sounds of the children in the alley. The thump thump, thump thump went on rhythmically from the tatami next door. She looked up at the off-white patch of ceiling that was the lens cover on her universe. The gentle, loving voice still sang within her. He knows me, loves me, sees me. I am living.

A thin edge of guilt penetrated her reflections. But

62

what of Keiko? She had looked so tired and wan in the light of early morning and she had been so anxious to rush off and visit her aunt in Ueno without even asking Harumi to accompany her. Then, like a fleeting break in a dark sky, she saw Keiko's flushed face and recalled the intensity of her feelings. Poor Keiko. How desperately she must have wanted the dream to continue.

Waiting to cross the seaside road at Kamakura Michiko said to herself: it's not like it was on television. Nothing ever is. It's only when you're in the picture yourself that you discover the dust, the noise and the smells. The glittering cavalcade of traffic separating her from the seashore was slowing. When the next convoy of tourist buses pulled up to spill out its cargo the traffic would stop altogether. Then she would be able to thread her way through the tight hot metal and feel the breath of the sea.

On the express from Tokyo she had stood all the way thinking of sea and sand and the rise and fall of the waves. The train was fevered with anticipation of the seashore. She had been caught up in the excitement, rushing toward a new experience, not enclosed by the everlasting walls made by man. Kamakura must truly be a splendid place. Why else was everybody so eagerly seeking its shore that day?

Michiko wore a new, light blue cotton dress which she had chosen with the heat in mind for its simple low neckline and short sleeves. But the dress and the nylon close to her skin seemed to combine to package her and squeeze the sweat from her body. Even with the sunglasses she wore, the light relfecting from the burnished glass and metal hurt her eyes. Noise and strong light, she had found after only a short while in Tokyo, were the worst hazards in the daylight hours of a bar hostess.

At last the traffic came to a stop. Picking her way slowly between the vehicles Michiko felt the unfriendly eyes behind the glass. So many overheated faces staring, overheated minds fuming in the stop-start tension of Sunday driving. In the middle of the road she almost panicked; there was not enough space between cars to get through. But she found a gap in the chromium barricade and finally made her way to the other side.

As the traffic began to roar away behind her there was still no clear vista of the sea. It must be there somewhere, she thought, beyond the souvenir shops, seaside cafes and people seething around them. She knew it was there because she had seen it on television a few days earlier, the beautiful, sparkling blue-green sea of Kamakura and the laughing, shouting, suntanned bodies frolicking in it.

On the sea breeze the smell of hamburgers, hot dogs, curried rice and Kentucky fried chicken came in hot pungent waves. The crowd thickened. Everyone seemed in such a hurry eating and drinking and buying souvenirs, perhaps more even than on weekdays. There was a great deal of noise but little laughter.

Michiko made her way through the crowd and between two cafes found a ramp leading to the beach. The ramp was as busy as Meiji shrine on the first three days of New Year. Elevation and the slow pace down gave Michiko's eyes first view of the shore. Except for a far away gleam near the horizon there was no sea. Where sea and sand would have been there was only a vast olive pink mantle of bodies. By now she was coming down to the shore. She shut her eyes briefly and looked again. Far out in front and to left and right the carpet seemed to have spread. In all her life she had never dreamed of so many people on earth. But to choose to be crammed together on a hot Sunday afternoon in the same confined space . . . she had journeyed too far to try to battle her way back up the ramp.

At the bottom of the ramp there was a turmoil of bodies struggling to and from the shore. If she could believe her ears in the noise and confusion there was also an amplified male voice roaring for everyone whether in the sea or on the shore to please stand up and make room for more.

At the bottom of the ramp Michiko stood hemmed in on a multi-coloured carpet of orange peel and candy wrappers. She felt exhausted and on the verge of tears and in the same breath a desire to laugh in the face of the crowd. Why not pushers, she thought, like those at the big metropolitan stations in rush hour. They could push and push and keep on pushing until everyone was far out in the sea. That would solve a few problems.

The multitude of near nude bodies encompassed every age from the cradle to death's door, every shape, size and shade from lightest ivory and pink to dark mahogany. How much more realistic it would be if her clients could come to the White Bear clad only in those bulging little shorts. In the close thickets of flesh she looked for the enjoying eyes of children. She always sought the comfort of children's faces on her outings, but the children she saw now were being tugged this way and that and many were crying.

On her way to the seashore Michiko had visited the famous Hachiman shrine of Kamakura. She had intended to toss a good luck coin into the offering box and to make a wish. The forecourt was packed with tour buses and on the way up the crowded shrine steps she suddenly found herself behind a party of foreign tourists. The great rumps and heavy, slow turning faces infuriated her. While Richard Mayne's stature was less bulky and conspicuous than the tourists, she could not help linking his hateful foreignness with their presence.

Inside the shrine, still tucked behind the tour party, she suddenly recalled Mayne's homecoming early that morning. She was lying beside snoring Ishibashi on the very edge of sleep herself when Mayne mounted the courtyard and began to fumble with his keys and door. He was humming a tune, not overloud, but with an irritating good humour for that time of night. Later, inside the apartment he had knocked over a chair and this brought Ishibashi instantly awake.

Ishibashi was angry at being awakended and in some

strange man's way seemed to hold her responsible. When she tried to caress him back to sleep he became aroused and insisted on making love in an exotic Chinese position which stretched her legs interminably and curved her back like a bow. Penetration was so deep and lasting she thought she would die. It was all the fault of the foreigner, Richard Mayne, Mr Cat's Piss.

Michiko had turned from the shrine and made her way back down the steps. Meeting the foreigners was an omen. The rest of the day would be off key. Now, as she looked out drearily over the seascape of massed bodies, she thought of Ishibashi. It was his gangster's day off and he would be out with his wife and daughter Sunday driving in his big black car. Yes, it's Sunday after all, Michiko, thought, my day of rest and relaxation. She turned her face from the beach and began to thread her way slowly back up the ramp.

The chirping of countless insects and birds and the yelping of puppies acted like celestial music to Noguchi's far flying mind. A metre or so away, their heads close to the tiny cages, his two sons were examining a new stock of large flying beetles from the Tango peninsula. The boys were already tiring of the pair of budgerigars they had bought only last month and insisted that the beetles, which in flight made noises like small bombers, were now what they wanted.

The request for a visit to the department store had come from Yoshi, the older boy, at the precise moment when Noguchi's wife was about to begin the inquest into yet another of her husband's lost Saturdays. A secret smile glowed as Noguchi recalled the magical dissolution of his hangover. Within minutes he and his sons had scampered from the house and were moving down the road toward the station.

Sunday, Noguchi pondered, looking at his sons, in Mayne's language I could convert it to the day of my sons.

66

Every Sunday from morning till night I can watch my sons grow. When Yoshi turns away from the beetles and straightens his body he will be taller than I and in only a few more Sundays Tomo will be level with me. Then they will both grow taller and stronger as I begin to shrink.

The boys' slender bodies were clad in tight blue jeans and white T-shirts. On his Sunday outings with the boys Noguchi felt alternately elated and downcast. With the voice of a Shinjuku barker, to anyone who would listen, he sometimes wished to cry: look, here are my two sons. Look well. See their fine stature and bright eyes? They are the future of Japan, the hope of the world.

Then, in a shop mirror, he would catch his own reflection, the greying temples, stubby arms and legs, plump torso and ever-broadening face and he would see himself as of another species, an ancient bumbling penguin, an old wobbly bear. At such moments he was glad the boys now walked apart from him, engrossed in the preoccupations of their own age and time.

The creatures, large and small, regardless of the bars and cages, poured all their song through the wide doors and out on to the department store roof where it dispersed in the vaporous heights of the city. Noguchi, looking at his sons, thought: they are strangers, it is only an illusion that I could ever know them. We are as separate as the bars on the cages. If I were to walk to the elevator now and drop out of their world they would scarcely notice. Tomorrow morning, first thing, my wife would telephone my president asking polite questions about my company pension. That is all.

Noguchi's back was against a bright yellow wall near one of the roof entrances. The space in front of him was crushed with sweating Sunday fathers and the pride and joy of their week. The children chirped their questions like crickets, misting the eyes of the fathers into half forgotten images of childhood insects. Actors, Noguchi thought, like me. Look at him, the very thin one there with the plump little boy, hear his special Sunday father's voice:

67

"When I was a little boy in Fukuoka the flying beetles were so big and fast they made holes as big as rice bowls in our paper screens . . . ."

Nature bought and sold on a roof top in the sky. Noguchi looked closely at the animated faces of the customers young and old. Nothing was strange, bizarre, beyond the mind's reach any more. When I was a boy (he tuned the interior voice so that it would in no way be reminiscent of his father's), when I was a boy everywhere I went insects chirped and buzzed and hopped and flashed their wings in the sky. Now they are little more than merchandise to be bought and sold like toys and rice cakes. The only insects in my daily life are cockroaches. He glanced again at the customers' swarming shining eyes. How they would laugh if he expressed himself aloud.

His sons were still peering into the beetle cages. He traced the line of Yoshi's arched body, almost fifteen, already in his second year of high school. He noted the long energetic legs, the fine shoulders and arms. Even in his crouched position the boy swayed and pivoted constantly like a boxer. How soon would Yoshi's body seek to shed its chrysaline restraints, to move ahead, free of the dreary commonsense yoke of mother and father. Perhaps, thought Noguchi, he has escaped already.

His eyes moved from Yoshi to a gap in the mist of his own boyhood. He was walking in a narrow backstreet in a small southern city, passing a row of tiny houses enclosed by wooden fences. A woman in a bright blue kimono, sitting framed in a window. The vibrant evening voice cooing: "Ah, what's such a handsome boy doing in this city alone and on such a lovely calm evening?"

Startled, he gazed this way and that seeking the invisible focus of the woman's attention. She can't mean me. At last he looked into the window frame and stammered, "I, I . . . well I, I . . . ."

He had graduated from high school only a few weeks earlier and was visiting the city for the first time on an errand for his employer. No woman had ever spoken to

68

him like that before.

"Ah, I can see from your eyes you are a poet. You will write lovely haiku and tanka one day." She had left the window now and was opening the little gate for him. "Please come in and be with me for a while. Such a handsome boy. Please."

The woman's face, not old, not young, was the image of a renowned woodblock print. Her white powdered cheeks were as round as toy balloons. Over her forehead splashes of hair like black enamel lay. Her eyebrows were arched like the wings of a tiny black bird and her lips were coral pink. And the eyes, he sucked in his breath, so dark and deep yet so bold and giving. The only feature to set the face apart from the woodblock print was the absence of a toothpick between the lips.

He followed the woman into the house. There was an unknown heady perfume in the aura of her body. "Yes, the handsome boy will one day write splendid poetry. Now please don't be shy of me. I too am an artist in my own modest way." She served green tea from a pot on a small lacquered table. He felt his flesh like an unruly landed fish on the warm tatami.

Somehow the quilt had tangled itself around his legs. He could still feel the imprint of her lips all over his body. His penis ached and his mouth was dry, and poems cool and happy would not stop igniting in his mind. "Will the handsome boy write a haiku for me and bring it back one day?"

That night, on his way home in the train, he wrote in his notebook, "Why must money change hands for a glimpse of one's origin. It is like paying to look at the sun and the moon." A few days later the Pacific war broke out. He never saw the woman again.

"Look father, look." In the lee of Yoshi's smiling face Tomo was holding up a tiny barred cage from which a long feeler protruded limply.

Noguchi acted out a show of interest with his eyes and prepared a little homily for the creature encaged. But his eyes would not focus on the dim barred smudge and it

69

seemed as many years passed by as he had devoted to his company before he overheard his voice at last saying, "Well, yes, it is alive as we are. We must take good care of it."

When Kato was talking, and he talked most of the time, Mayne rarely ventured an interruption. Ever since his first visit three years earlier Kato's shrill voice had been climbing higher. Now, facing the phrenetic gyrations of the fan and the barrage of hot words, Mayne almost wished the pulsing time-bomb in his head would go off.

"You think I am not going crazy listening all day to those fools. The other day my old English professor was talking about a visit to London in 1955." Kato's eyes were glittering. "He was telling us about his visits to the Albert Hall, the British Museum and Westminster. I wanted to shout at him, what's that word you taught me, ah so, nitwit. You crazy old nitwit, you've bored us with that four times this month already. I looked round the class. Only three of the others were awake."

Kato puffed clouds of smoke into the turbulent air. Mayne watched the smoke swirling like a mini cyclone as it caught the force of the fan. Mostly, on his sporadic visits Kato was as welcome as a charge of fresh air. If only he would turn the volume down, Mayne thought, just for a moment. "I am not your old English professor," he said. "You know I went to Shinjuku last night. Please have some consideration for the state of my mind."

A superb sneer peeled back Kato's lips. "It is the generation gap," he hissed, "and I know it is in the west as here. I have read about it. Every day while the crazy old professors dream about the past the gap widens."

A wave of compassion softened Mayne's irritation. On the telephone Kato had told him he had passed the entrance examination for Mitsubishi Heavy Industries; on March 31 next year the four liveliest years of Kato's existence would come to an end. He would put away his books and his jeans and have his hair cut to a salary

70

man's level. The following day in a new dark suit and tie junior administration clerk Kato would find his desk in the clockwork belly of the giant company. Let the anger burn brightly now, Mayne thought; soon the spirit will be ash.

"Can't you see," Kato exclaimed, "if I said Tokyo Tower was falling down you would be shocked, would not believe me, yet while we sit here and talk the whole structure of our human world is falling down so fast. Since I was old enough to remember, can you imagine the changes my eyes have seen? Now the pace grows faster while my professors are still living in the dark."

"Yes," Mayne said, "I have heard many voices in Japan. I can understand your feeling." In the beginning he had hesitated to fit the word beautiful to Kato's image but as time passed he could find no other more appropriate word. The superb, deep-chested body and splendid mind and the fire and intelligence of the eyes formed an almost unique combination in Mayne's view. Only the shrill, sometimes childlike disparity of Kato's voice tempered his perfection. While the quick fire words made patterns in Mayne's mind he was thinking: with all his strength, how can the human mechanism be expected to absorb the changes demanded of him. Poor Kato. The biggest shock of all for him is still to come.

"Then from all those voices what have you learned of our inner feelings," Kato demanded, "the so called Japanese way. Do you know what is in the mind of every elitist Japanese salary man as he walks in the streets of Ginza? Can you answer me, my teacher?"

The use of "teacher" nearly raised a laugh in Mayne. In the early days there had been a few ludicrous English conversation lessons and when these came to an end Kato had offered Mayne Japanese lessons, but as the level of Kato's exasperation rose these too were dropped.

Now they met casually a few times a year in the apartment or bars and coffee shops. At last Mayne said, trying to sound as if he really did not know, "Enlighten me then, what are these Japanese salary men thinking as they walk in Ginza?"

Kato widened his eyes and gazed into space like a seer. "Every elitist salary man in the streets of Ginza is thinking of a beautiful white Caucasian woman with milky white skin and golden blond hair. She is like the centrefold of Playboy, only that most treasured part which is blacked out in the Playboy he sees is now like a neon sign in his head. There is nothing else in his mind except that beautiful white body and blond hair and that word you taught me . . . fuck. . . . His salary man's suit is gone. Mitsubishi, Mitsui and Sumitomo have no meaning anymore. All his energy and ambition is centred in the beautiful white body and golden blond hair."

Mayne laughed. "So that's what it comes to then. All the concrete, glass, steel and plastic is only the background for the rampant male animal. Perhaps we would be better off if we returned to the real jungle." A flush like a rosy dawn crept into Kato's face. It was a state that was induced unfailingly whenever sex was mentioned. Puffs of nervous smoke flew in the air. "It is true," he said crossing his legs, "so many years of severe discipline and education at top universities and it all ends in a mind full of fuck in Ginza. Or did you once teach me fuck all, nothing?" He burst out laughing.

Mayne laughed too. There was an irresistable contagion in Kato's sudden changes of mood. "Congratulations from this very bad teacher. You have an excellent memory for four-letter words. But seriously . . . no matter what happens in Ginza now you are a product of four thousand years continuous civilisation. Many times you have come to me with bouquets of flowers delicately arranged by your own hands. In most western countries few men are brave enough to carry flowers in public and fewer still capable of arranging them. The commerce of Ginza has little to do with ancient traditions of beauty and delicacy."

The flush had left Kato's face. In a lighter, calmer voice he said, "What matter if I love flowers and see beauty in the limbs and leaves of trees and the colour of ripening

72

fruit. My eyes see and my mind translates but my life is controlled by the old professors and the ethics of Ginza."

From the alley Mayne heard the faint sound of water trickling. Feet were slapping quickly across the tatami in the apartment above. By now his mattress on the bamboo pole would be streaked with dirty laundry water. It was too late to act; the damage was done. Trivia, he told himself, fighting the rising pulse of his feelings. He sighed. "At least we have the illusion sometimes of making our own way."

Kato stood up abruptly. "Now is my playing time. My friends are waiting for me in Shinjuku." He gave a shy smile. "Sometimes I am troublesome I know. Thank you for listening to me." He glanced at the bruise on Mayne's forehead. "Please take care of your head."

When Kato's footsteps had faded Mayne took a cloth and went to the alley. The mattress was so blotched with laundry water that he could do little with it. He turned back to the tatami, took off his clothes and lay down. The swelling on his forehead had gone down considerably but his temple still throbbed. He shut his eyes. If like counting sheep he tried to fill in all the gaps of last night sleep must come.

He recalled leaving Tarugoya, loud voices in the street, black uniforms swarming and the Waseda song, pavement fortune tellers and lightning artists busy in shop doorways, a yellow stream of taxis . . . the image of Harumi . . . .

Overhead the baby began to cry. Swift footsteps whispered on the tatami. A lullaby began, low and gentle. Mayne smiled and settled himself for sleep.

All that day at the bank the commerce of Harumi's activity flowed like a dream. Every face, shade of cloth and document was clearer, sharper. She had read somewhere that certain drugs induced altered states of consciousness and heightened perception. This is how it must be, she thought, as her fingers winged over the keyboard and the English words expanded like magic on the paper. She smiled to herself. My drug must be top secret.

In the changing room during lunch break an older woman in her section laid her hands on Harumi's arms and drew her close. The eyes looking into her were quizzical, the mouth half smiling. In a few moments the hands withdrew and the smile came to full flower. The eyes, in after image, said: I know your secret and in a way I envy you. But there is no need for words.

Other members of her section, while praising her appearance, said there was something different about her, a subtle change that puzzled them. In turn she found them more agreeable and the whole day passed without grievance or pettiness. Even her section chief, stroking his chin and gazing at her with rare intensity, commended her work and her brightness.

On the rush hour train from Shibuya, in the sweating embrace of countless bodies, Harumi thought wistfully of a hot bath and change of clothes. It was rather childish, she realised, but she wanted her body to be as fresh and immaculate as the brand new bank notes in the envelope in her handbag. When the cashier at the bank handed her the bank notes she had wrapped them carefully in rice paper and placed them in a fresh white envelope. It was ironical, she thought, that while the bank notes remained immaculate she, the human bearer, was buffeted and shoved like an animal on the way to slaughter.

She was grateful though that the usual rush hour sex touchers did not seem to be near her. The crowding bodies pinned her arms to her sides leaving her so vulnerable that if any hand had sought to violate her she would have been powerless to prevent it. She had been touched so much on rush hour trains that the feelings of outrage and shame had been gradually tempered to weary resignation. This evening, however, it would have been an intolerable violation of her spirit as well as her body.

Walking up the street toward Mayne's apartment Harumi discovered she was a little early for her

74

appointment. She was approaching a little park, cool and inviting, which she had noticed with pleasure on her first visit. The perfect place, she thought, as she crossed the gravel and sank down gratefully on the bench under the silver birch.

From the apartment complexes on the hump of hill behind her and the houses clustered on the other side of the street a medley of television channels clashed in the dinnertime air. At the end of their long hot day the curves and spines of the reclining monsters seemed jaded. How odd, Harumi thought, I hardly ever notice such things. I seem to have been wandering in the dark for years.

Familiar cooking smells proliferated and separated themselves in her mind. She remembered the little Chinese restaurant further up the street from which Mayne told her he sometimes ordered meals. Although Harumi dined by herself most evenings it troubled her to think of Mayne eating his evening meal alone. To her mind he was like the trees and shrubs in the park, an exotic island in a vast colourless sea.

A little boy in a bright red shirt and black shorts ran down the street and into the park. Without glancing at Harumi he climbed on to the only swing and set it moving. Soon the little black and red pendulum was hazing back and forth against the pale blue sky. As he swung he was humming a children's song, which Harumi also knew, from Hokkaido. Seeing boy and swing and sky blending Harumi thought: how small and solitary he looks up there in the sky yet how much a part of the spinning world.

The envelope lay unopened beside the appointment book. Harumi sipped a glass of peach juice. "I see you have your dictionary and diary," Mayne said. "Good. Just relax for a while. I guess it's been a long day." There was not a trace of the day's heat on her. The burnt orange blouse she wore looked as if it was fresh from a boutique hanger and its wearer from the bathhouse. Mayne touched his weakly throbbing forehead. Be convinced, he told himself, like you, she is human.

He saw the look in her briefly raised eyes. "Yes, well," he said, "as I told you on the telephone, I do not really know how it happened. Shinjuku has a strange effect on me. Whenever I go there my memory seems to turn itself off. Perhaps it's just as well." He raised the appointment book and slid the envelope underneath.

When Harumi first caught sight of the dark bruise on his pale forehead it had startled her. She could almost feel his pain. "In Shinjuku," she agreed, "many strange things happen. We sometimes overdrink and overenjoy ourselves there."

Mayne grinned. "By the way I feel today I must have done at least one of those things last night. But what an unworthy teacher I am sitting here talking about my bad habits." He glanced at the diary. "There is so much I want to hear about your daily life. Shall we begin? Just take your time."

Harumi opened the diary and began to read. "'On Saturday afternoon I met Mr Mayne in his apartment. We discussed my English lessons. At last Mr Mayne agreed to teach me English conversation one night a week. I was so happy.'" She continued reading, translating as she went the exotic words and sounds into her mind's language. Now and then Mayne stopped her to offer minor corrections.

"'After leaving Mr Mayne's apartment I met my friend Keiko at Hachiko in Shibuya. We went to my friend's apartment and ate dinner together. Later we listened to classical music and then we drank a little whisky. We talked about many things and went to bed about 1am. . . .'"

As Harumi was turning the page Mayne said, "Did you talk to your friend Keiko about coming to me for English lessons?" For a moment he held the image of the two radiant faces coming together at Hachiko.

"Yes," Harumi said after a pause, resentful of the telltale glow in her face. "She is my intimate friend. We talk about everything."

The tacit understanding as their eyes met was as clear as if she had just recounted every word of her conversation with Keiko. He knows without words, she thought. It was like communicating on two levels at the same time, one the halting, superficial tongue, the other unspoken, but instantly and subtly understood.

"'I got up at seven o'clock this morning,'" Harumi went on. "'After breakfast I took a bus to my office. It was my first experience to have no problems at my office in one whole day. Everyone smiled at me and even my section chief was kind. I feel so happy; soon I will go to Mr Mayne's apartment.' That is all," she said, closing the diary.

Mayne grinned. "That tells me just about everything," he said, "but please call me Richard. Mr makes me feel like the oldest foreigner in Tokyo."

All day Michiko stayed on her bed smoking cigarettes, not wanting to move. It was Monday, not just another blue Monday but one more long gap between her and her time at the White Bear. This is reality, she told herself, and gave a little laugh, the reality of the daily life of a bar hostess in Tokyo.

The English word 'honeymoon' came to her lips; it was often used in the language of her bar. When the honeymoon is over . . . smiles all round and much sardonic laughter. Only the other night a client had said, "The honeymoon is the dream, its aftermath reality."

The telephone had not rung all day. Through the vibrant walls like a seashell cupped to the ear the sound of the city roared. If I got up and opened the door, Michiko thought, it would all come bursting in like a tidal wave. Tokyo, my lover, she breathed, and smiled to herself. How soon we tired of each other. The clock ticking endlessly beside the bed would tell her at last when it was time to open the door.

Once, in the late afternoon, she heard the foreigner whistling. Although the tune was unfamiliar there was no doubt of the irresponsible theme it conveyed. He has a lover, she thought, the foreigner has a lover. Foreigner. Lover. The words coupled were obscene. She shuddered. Imagine waking up one morning and finding those grey-green eyes staring at you out of that great white moon of a face.

The clock ticked: Michiko, Michiko, Michiko, Michiko, Michiko. She glanced at it. Horror. She would be late. There was no time to bathe. A few splashes of cold water here and there and a mouthful of tepid green tea would suffice. She pulled on her clothes, straightened seams, and felt the sweat beginning. She jingled the keys from her bag.

The door slammed behind her like a thunderclap. Clattering over the courtyard she could not avoid the open window and the candid interior of the foreigner's apartment. The fleeting image of him bending over drying his porcelain buttocks with a pink towel, the impression in sharp natural colour, sped with her down the steps and all the way to the main road. It was as well the donkey part had been obscured. A blue Monday was bad enough, never mind such a barbaric spectacle as that.

Michiko waited by the crossing at the plaza for a gap to open in the sea of traffic. On the other side of the street a line of upraised arms signalled taxis. The lights changed, converting the traffic flow to two hypertensively opposed columns, snarling and choking to be on the way again. She hurried through the gap and positioned herself on the other side of the street a few metres in front of a middle-aged housewife in kimono.

Mindful of the housewife's agitated skyward arm Michiko smiled to herself, watch this. In a few moments a taxi pulled up beside her and the door flew open. As Michiko swung her legs over the back seat she caught the anger in the eyes of the housewife. Then the country-boy kamikaze driver was smiling at her through the mirror.

"Late for the bar, I imagine," he grinned. "Leave it to me." And they were speeding away, passing other angry eyes and frustrated signals.

Taxi rides were the one passion of Michiko's time in Tokyo that had not failed. On the worst days, even on the way to work, the incredible bursts of speed and unbelievable near misses thrilled her. She sat back in the seat, her thighs crossed, holding her breath while the taxi bucked and hurtled through the air like a roller coaster. At the railway bridge, near the gut of Shibuya, the taxi seemed for moments on end to have entered the sky. Then in the next breath the motor was ticking sedately opposite the lit up sign of the White Bear.

Akiyama was a regular Monday night client. Michiko had never understood why he chose her. He was a Tokyo-born insurance clerk, immaculate to the last burnished hair on his head, an economics graduate of Waseda University. From behind his splendid spectacles his eyes searched her with intense interest. "This one," he said, extending the photo, "please tell me what you think of this one Michiko?"

She took the photo and studied it carefully. It showed a young woman in a white dress standing in front of a cherry tree in blossom. The face looked like countless other faces Michiko could see in Tokyo streets any day she wished. "Well . . . I think she looks rather cute. How old is she by the way?"

Akiyama fiddled with the gold band of his watch. "She is 29 but her father is president of a middle-sized pickle company in Yokohama. They have a large family home in Ueno I understand."

"Please excuse me but I have forgotten, how old are you now?" Michiko had not forgotten but she liked to expand her Monday nights with Akiyama. She still held the photo close, examining it in appropriate moments as if all her energies were flowing into the figure in the white dress.

Akiyama sipped his moderate beer. "I am 37. She is a

79

graduate of Ohtsuma Women's University and speaks a little English I believe. But don't you think just a little . . . she has radish legs?"

Michiko held the photo closer, masking the giggle trembling on her lips. Foolish man, she thought, of course she has radish legs; so do I. Does he wish to marry only a pair of slim legs? She looked up and said in a confident voice, "Just a little, a very little, but she looks a nice lady to me."

Although she was aware of Akiko just two booths away Michiko picked up her whisky on the rocks and took a comfortable drink. Akiyama was mild and well mannered and his bill could always be padded a few thousand yen. The pitch of enthusiasm in his voice had begun to rise. "Don't you think the two of us in Hibiya Park would look, well . . . sharp together?"

"Yes, really sharp, a fine pair, I feel certain." In fact Machiko could not distinguish between this photo and the one he had brought the previous week and all the other photos he had shown her before that. "But what happened to the one you showed me last week? Sumiko wasn't it?"

A cloud of sadness briefly dimmed Akiyama's eyes. "Well, I don't quite know how to say it. It's a delicate matter and I know the weather is so terribly hot but she had a . . . peculiar odour." He wrinkled his nose. "I thought it would go away but it followed us everywhere we went in Ginza."

Michiko pressed her face close to the photo. Within her anger and laughter bubbled. If she herself went to the marriage agency, what would the computer select for her? A Shinjuku pimp? A fish slicer? A garbage man? She flashed a bright encouraging smile at Akiyama. "Never mind, I'm sure this one will be more suitable. She has a very gentle face." She handed back the photo.

As she had seen him many times before, Akiyama sat enthralled like a race track gambler poring over a tipping sheet. She could feel the enthusiasm mounting to its climax. Soon he would look up beaming and at last he would exclaim, "Yes, Michiko, I know it for certain, this is the real one. Already I can hear the wedding march . . . ."

From the corner of her eye Michiko saw Ishibashi enter the bar and start down the aisle toward Akiko's booth. She bowed her head to her drink. A pulse began throbbing in her neck. Akiyama raised his head. His eyes were shining. "Yes," he said, "Oh yes Michiko, at last, the wedding march . . . ."

The diary lay open on the desk. In the desk light's glow the dark columns of symbols sprang vividly to life from Noguchi's pen. The point had been reached where the moving pen was no longer in his control. His eyes were now beyond the pen and the page following an endless ribbon of images.

"I stood in the temple garden," he wrote, "beside a small shrine wherein a Buddha carved in wood was raised on a block of stone. On the face of the Buddha I saw the hand of the maker. On the earth, beneath the pointing shards of its arm the hand of the Buddha lay. Between the fingers, brown like old leaves, a green bamboo shoot was rising . . . ."

Noguchi put down the pen and stood up. Through the glass panels the unlit desks in the outer office looked as solemn and lifeless as tombstones. How long did I spend out there, he wondered. How many lives? He walked to his office door then back to the desk. Behind him through the dull grey wall the factory was silent.

He sat down in happy contemplation, of liberated thoughts and secret dreams. "I am Noguchi, poet, businessman. Here I can say it aloud." And he heard his wife's voice from afar, petulant. "Where is he, oh where is he, my never-come-home Jekyll and Hyde husband?"

In his years in the outer office and all the other offices in the chain of his company's command Noguchi had yearned for privacy. The more confined the space, the closer the jostling desks, eyes, hands, the happier his colleagues were, while he remained, strangled by

81

proximity, pursuing the destiny of millions of plastic buttons, never able once to open his mouth and breathe a word of the inner mind.

Then, after a particularly severe spring bonus offensive when his desk was surrounded for days by infuriated union activists it was decided that Noguchi should be enclosed in an office of his own. The top half, his president declared, would be in glass and the lower section pannelled in plastic mahogany. Accommodated in this manner Noguchi would not be shut away like some remote god, nor on the other hand exposed to the world like an object in a glass case. If he stood up he could see and be seen by the outer office. Seated, he was in a world entirely of himself.

Noguchi took a key from his pocket and unlocked his private drawer. The time was coming when he must clear it out, but while they remained its contents were treasured layers of his memory. His hands sifted the treasures. Hemingway's "Old Man and the Sea" half read, Dostoyevsky's "Crime and Punishment", tattered scraps of childhood poetry still legible, a faded oval portrait of his mother, the book of Basho grey and worn, an envelope of erotic prints purchased in a drunken moment in Shinjuku, a personal bank passbook and countless cards for bars, bath houses and cafes . . . . During the day, when the factory hummed through the wall and the outer office palpitated with its activities, he only had to unlock the drawer to find the other world.

Noguchi locked the drawer and swung back into position over the diary. In the short time since he had stopped reading the diary to Mayne he was able to write more freely. He used his own language now and there was no one to look over his shoulder and try to apprehend his meaning. He positioned the point of the pen on the paper and watched the word symbols begin. "That day, in my mother's house, I remember it was terribly hot . . . .

"My elder sister, a primary school teacher in a nearby city, had been staying with us that weekend and was due soon to depart. At times during the heat of the afternoon I

82

heard my mother and sister quarrelling fretfully. Several times I heard my mother saying that my sister's university education had turned her into a revolutionary.

"There was also a young man, a middle school teacher in our town, lodging in my mother's house. He was tall and very thin and had a face that always seemed to be in shadow. That afternoon I recall, and I cannot say now why it still remains so clear, the face of my mother's lodger seemed even less happy.

"We walked along the road, the four of us, toward the coach depot, the yellow dust puffing out all around us in quick, new-born clouds. I walked with the lodger, who stared ahead of him constantly and said not a single word. In front, my mother and sister walked, my mother in her best dark grey Sunday kimono, my sister in a long blue skirt and rose pink blouse. I had never seen anyone dressed like my sister in our town before.

"From behind screens and garden shrubs I could feel the eyes of our neighbours on us. The voices whispered inside my head: look at her in her fine western clothes. She is a teacher now I understand and also, I hear, a, a red. All the way to the coach station the eyes of the watchers contorted my self-conscious body like a puppet's jig.

"At the coach station my sister was about to climb on board when she suddenly exclaimed to the lodger: 'My parasol, I have forgotten it. Please run to my mother's house and fetch it while I wait.'

"Without a word the lodger immediately began the long run to our home. The dust rose after him, I recall, like great yellow mushrooms exploding from the earth. Soon my mother's lodger was obscured from our view.

"In what seemed only a few moments I was astonished to see the lodger returning again down the road. He came to us covered in sweat and dust from head to toe and carrying the parasol like a blazing torch. As he drew near, the coach driver loudly announced that the coach was about to depart.

"My sister climbed on to the open back of the coach

and sat smiling down on the lodger. He moved forward, holding out the trophy to her. 'Here is your parasol,' he said humbly.

"In a gesture superbly matching the imperious nature of her smile my sister waved her arm. 'Take it back,' she commanded, 'take it back to my mother's house. I have no need of it now.' And with the last brilliant flash of her smile the coach rumbled off into the dust.

"For some time the young man stood looking after the coach, the parasol drooping in his hand now like a dead flower. What, I wondered, was passing through his mind as he began the long, slow walk back to our house on that hot Sunday afternoon . . . ."

The long alley to L'Ambre coffee lounge was slimed with fish scales and dirty water and studded with overflowing garbage cans. Mayne walked a little ahead taking in the chaos of smells and sounds from the row of busy cafe kitchens. To pass into the street on the other side of the alley where the cage fronts sparkled was like moving into another country. There in the windows the lucky cats beckoned and the smell of the food was delightful.

Sometimes before entering L'Ambre Mayne made a circuit of the cafes, back and front, marvelling at the gap between the civilised side with its come-in smiles and spick and span facades and the shambles of the alley at the rear. Only a few metres separated the two extremes. It was the essence of the city, of all cities, one side glitter and promise, the other decaying reality.

Mayne opened the door of L'Ambre and moved aside to let Harumi enter. Rachmaninov's Second Concerto, in courageous stereophonic sound, throbbed through the gloom. They climbed the narrow stairs to the third level and found a booth. Harumi sat on the inner side feeling the spirit of L'Ambre coming to life in the near darkness. The high-backed double chair they shared, draped with its white headcloth, was like an old fashioned airliner

84

seat. It stood, one of a row, facing the obscure point in the distance from where the sound of Rachmaninov came.

Harumi turned to Mayne. "How did you find such a coffee shop in Tokyo? Before tonight I thought such places only existed in fantasy."

"If you look for it," he said, "Tokyo has everything, every food, drink and entertainment, everything for the needs of the mind, body and spirit, good, bad and mediocre according to taste. Sometimes, though, I think it was L'Ambre that found me." From the almost invisible waiter he ordered coffee. "When the city has drained all my energy I come here and sit in the dark and relax." It was perfectly natural for Mayne to be whispering to Harumi. Voices took little part in the atmosphere of L'Ambre.

She could still barely make out his eyes. "I am surprised," she said, and hesitated, "when I look at you, you are foreign but when I see you you are not foreign at all. I hope you understand me. It's so strange." The build-up of good feelings from the day gave impetus to her candour. What can I fear, she thought, I have only my body and its vague impressions to lose. If he is love then how can I be afraid?

Ravel's Bolero had taken over from Rachmaninov. Although the sound of music dominated, Harumi was slowly becoming aware of the presence of other people, a dim figure moving silently past the booth, voices whispering somewhere ahead and the subtle clink of china. Mayne said, "Sometimes they sit here for hours and mostly in silence. At first I used to think they were waiting for friends and lovers like the people over there in the square of Hachiko. They are lonely — that is easy to tell — but they are all linked together by the music."

"Are you lonely?" She was aware of his hand now, close and still on the table beside her. At the climax of the Bolero the sensation of that hand moving on her body came with impish satisfaction in her mind. "Excuse me," she murmured, "I am trying to say does being a foreigner sometimes make you lonely?"

85

"No, not any more in Japan. It might seem strange to you but in Auckland, New York or London with my language all around me I could feel much more alone than here." Involuntarily he put his hand over hers. "To live, to breathe, to look in a mirror is to be alone. I guess in that sense we are all foreign and separate."

The spontaneous thrill of his hand invoked sharp images of Keiko's eyes and voice. "Foreign men are cunning. He will take you step by step like a little mountain trout." The words came as from a dream but the warning glowed in Keiko's eyes. Harumi indulged in a secret, guiltless smile. If only Keiko could see into her at this moment how shocked and angry she would be.

In the enclosure of his hand Mayne felt the warm fingers turn and twine. A Mozart flute concerto had just begun. Its haunting purity seeped slowly into him almost as if he were vibrating within the core of the instrument itself. They sat without speaking, coming down only occasionally to sip their coffee and glance into one another. At last she said, "Tonight I seem to have forgotten the meaning of time. I think my first lesson now is over."

The warmth of her smile was in her voice. As much to himself as to Harumi, Mayne said, "I think my first lesson is just beginning. Long may it last."

They stood up, tracing the smooth wood of the balcony to the curve of the stairs. Going down, Harumi was able to turn and implant the surreal impact of L'Ambre. The three shrouded galleries hung from the high wall as if welded there by the sound of music. There were vague mesmeric shapes of people seated motionless and the dull gloss of dark heads resting on dark tables. It was life suspended in time like a picture gallery, she thought, strange and lonely and so at peace.

In the alley, now awash with the guts and bones of chickens and fish and overflowing vegetable scraps, they dodged and laughed and slithered like children. By the square of Hachiko they emerged holding hands and passed through the centre of the crowd waiting by the fountain and into the mouth of Shibuya station.

Michiko rolled over on the tatami and fluttered a handful of tissues from the box. The snapping flit flit sound echoed exactly the action on the well known television commercial, only the television commercial did not show where the tissues went after they left the box. How curious, Michiko thought, if 20 million people could see her bending to attend to Ishibashi's damp needs, then tucking a snowy handful between her own thighs.

She felt Ishibashi's eyes wide open in the lamp glow. It was rare for him to stay awake long after the act of love, especially when it was so late. But perhaps if she could nerve herself sufficiently it was a good time to approach him. She drew closer, embraced him lightly and snuggled her face on to his chest. There was nothing in the rise and fall of his flesh to indicate his mood. She would have to gamble on his recently spent energies inducing a calm response. Slowly she drew the question from its longstanding niche in her mind. "One day you said you would help to establish me in a bar. I am so anxious to be independent now. Is it possible to find me a small place?"

The soft plump hillocks that were Ishibashi's chest continued to rise and fall evenly. Except when he was very drunk or very angry Michiko had no indication of what was in his mind. While her hand lay gently sensing but not carressing the hollow of his neck and shoulder Michiko's ear was poised for the rumble that would soon begin to overshadow the heartbeat. As a little girl she sometimes lay in the long grass on the fringe of the paddy fields and listened to the language of the earth. Its mystical pulses sang reassuring songs in her ears, occasionally soothing her to sleep. Now at least Ishibashi's flesh was warm like her own and the hillocks were beginning to vibrate a response.

"Well, I was going to tell you, one of the syndicate's bars on the west side of Shinjuku, a good little place, will be available in a few months. The Moma-san is retiring because of ill health some time in the winter. Other members of the syndicate agree that you are most suitable to fill the position."

The rate of undulation in Ishibashi's hillocks was increasing. Whether it was because of the rare expenditure of words or for some other more fundamental reason Michiko was too overjoyed at that moment to consider. Little bar, my bar, little bar, little bar . . . .

Through the bulk of flesh beneath her eyes she saw the little bar taking shape, the soft light reflecting the mirrored elegance of her pale gold kimono — no more tart-like western clothers for her — Michiko herself in calm command enthroned in the wood pannelled enclosure of the number one booth attending the voice of a big-spending company man, keeping an eye and an ear all the while to the high-spirited antics of the two or three young hostesses in the other booths. My bar, my own little bar . . . .

Then gratitude to Ishibashi began to well in her. With all his bull-like ways he was the only man in the world to pay attention to her, and now this . . . She fought to control the tears that she knew he would not wish to see. The pillar of flesh seemed now lighter, warmer, almost affectionate. My bar, my own little bar. She could see the glitter like iced diamonds in Akiko's eyes.

As she recalled the unworthy thoughts of Ishibashi that had entered her mind from time to time guilt and shame filled Michiko like a poison. He is my man, my lover, my benefactor, he desires me. She opened her lips, extending her tongue to the tiny brown nipple so close and tempting. He is generous. I will give, give. She licked and tickled then took the nipple between her lips and sucked it and caressed it with darting movements of her tongue.

Ishibashi's voice rumbled up through the hillocks. "Show me that place, quick, quick."

She stood up quickly, got the vibrator from the cupboard and prepared herself for him. He lay on his side widening and raising her thighs and drawing his face close. While the patterns on the ceiling settled slowly into focus her hands, practised and unobtrusive, drew the curtains of her sex fully aside for him. The click of the vibrator switch punctuated his heavy breathing. Look well, big man, my lover, she breathed to the ceiling, I am ready, wanting.

The smooth, hard shape entered slowly, vibrating, teasing, thrusting, filling her with its unyielding palpitations. Ishibashi's eyes, the motivations of his hand, the faint liquid lap lapping of herself . . . were more exciting to Michiko than the to and fro of penetration. Open wider, there, he is fascinated, let him hear you. "Aah, it is good, so good . . . ."

She began to move for him — he liked that — and in a shallow space in the ceiling between two small beams the little paradise began to flower again. My own little bar, my own little bar. Whatever symbols glowed on the lighted bar sign outside she would change them to moon flower. It just came to her in the space between the beams as she began to move more excitedly for him and the lap lapping of herself grew more distinct. Moon flower. My own . . . .

Faintly, in the courtyard, Michiko heard the sound of footsteps and someone humming a tune. Then the foreigner's door opened and snapped shut softly like the closing of a book. She looked down. The white phallus was slipping from her. Ishibashi's face was set as in the mask of sleep, his breath coming harshly through moist half-opened lips. The eyes were strangely dazed like a child lost in a dream. She reached out and clasped the palpitant head of his sex. How he wants me, needs me, now.

"Move, move," the voice was rumbling. The hands clasping her buttocks were hurting. Then she was turning, kneeling, her hair draping the tatami, arching her back and moulding herself into the enclosure of his hips and thighs. He entered her slowly, his torso erect. He is gazing, I can feel him, slowly, all the way in and out again. Oh, how I clasp it, stiff, wet, bending, slowly, so tight.

Soon the deep sounds in his throat began. She joined him: "Iku, iku, iku, iku." But it seemed like the space between sunrise and dark before he at last was lying on her, full length, quivering, and the smooth clean sensation of the tatami was crushing her cheek and breast. My big man, my lover . . . .

Part 3

As he followed the twisting path higher Noguchi
smiled at the thought of the look that would have
darkened his president's face if he had simply said, "No, I
do not wish to go to the company lodge this weekend," the
shock shrinking the pupils of the president's eyes to
pinpoints, then the sparse figure expanding and trembling
into explosive anger. "How dare he, Noguchi the outsider,
have the affrontery to reveal his disloyalty in such a way."
If he had, from the beginning, refused all the company
picnics, seminars, excursions and lodge visits to Hakone
and Karuizawa what would have happened? The smile
broadened. Of course there would have been no
beginning in that case. Instead, his roving life, the life of a
true wanderer, would have begun so much earlier.
Perhaps he would be travelling somewhere in the forests
of Hokkaido or the highlands of Hakone as now, but free,
unfenced by time or obligation.

Noguchi stopped. On the edge of the path just beyond
him, a long green snake lay basking on a white rock.
Before slithering off into the undergrowth the snake
raised itself, conveying its recognition by a delicate
swaying of the head and upper body. "I think we met here
last year, or was it the year before," Noguchi murmured.
"Goodbye. Beware of mankind," and he walked on again

91

laughing softly.

Where were they now, his president and his colleagues? Standing on the countryclub golfcourse, no doubt, pointing to the highlands, still chuckling at the president's after dinner jibe last evening. Poor Noguchi, he may not know the difference between an eagle and a birdie but at least he never loses his balls . . . Isn't that his backside up there in the highlands as he peers at some mountain flower?

It did not matter to any of them that Noguchi had spent a lifetime with the company. The changing times only permitted them to laugh more openly now. Because of the ever widening gap he was unable to share with his colleagues mah jong and ping pong or even the electronic tension reducing equipment of the lodge. Nor could he have any part of the constant jibes and jokes that kept them linked together like mackerel in a school. The electronic revolution was burning out their guts, turning their minds into picture tubes and terminals. They needed each other sorely.

As the everyday land dwindled beneath him Noguchi began to think of Akamatsu and another mountain long ago.

Whenever he trod a mountain path, memory of Akamatsu returned. How many years had it been — eighteen, twenty? — since they had gone to the Southern Alps together that winter? What mountain range or back alley had at last claimed the spirit of his friend.

Before the trip to the southern alps Noguchi knew little of the life and thought of Akamatsu, little more than the evidence of the young man's withdrawn personality and the fact that he was labourer and a university graduate in the factory in which Noguchi was then employed. Somehow, in the course of their loneness and proximity, they had got talking and the tramping trip was conceived. Late on the afternoon of the first day while near the summit of their mountain a snow storm suddenly descended, cutting visibility to zero. Soon conditions were so bad that they were unable to risk movement in any

92

direction.

Noguchi felt an exhiliration, a finality, and he said to himself: there is no way out, soon I will die. And he became calm and clear headed and moments long buried in the span of his life flashed into his mind. It was as if all the points of his existence were drawing together on the mountainside.

In the face of the danger Akamatsu acted as if they were strolling on the gravel paths in the iris gardens of Meiji Park on a Sunday afternoon. He had them carefully construct a bivouac under a ledge of rock. Then they settled into their sleeping bags to wait the storm out. "There is no hurry," Akamatsu said, "we are well sheltered and we have no timetable here. The mountain will not abandon us."

Another mountain, Noguchi thought, another voice, and the words played back faithfully to him like a beloved record. The grade of the path was becoming more challenging, the humid air less sustaining. He paused and looked down. The carpet of green forest, the gateway to Edo, was seamed and random like a patchwork quilt. There was the long white gash of the motorway, the peeping walls, grey, brown and white of hotels, motels and lodges, the soft grey tiles of a surviving inn, and in the remote distance a faint yellow train snaking through a cutting.

In the far away drip dripping snow-dark space Akamatsu was saying, "The strike was long and difficult. There was no hope from the start. One by one other members of the union executive gave in. When it was over and all members had returned to work I was called to the office of the company president. He said to me, "Now you will never rise to a high position in this company or in any other important company in Japan'.""

The voice of Akamatsu was neither sad nor defeatist in that long-ago, wet, warm niche. "So from then, in all my free time, I began to climb mountains, always alone. The destiny of man is capricious. The status of the mountain remains unalterable."

A large, red dragon-fly zoomed from the undergrowth and went off nose-diving over the lip of the path. Where is Akamatsu now? How soon I lost contact with him after that mountain. For a long moment Noguchi stood suspended above the patchwork green forest, following the land to where the distant spines of ranges met the powder blue ocean of sky. Then, bracing his legs for the steeper climb, he set off slowly up the path like a sailor mounting a gangway.

The fan whined and dipped, spraying hot air in ever more fevered arcs. The typewriter sat on the table with the feet of a donkey, obstinately refusing the yield of a word. Several times that day across the courtyard Michiko's slamming door had rattled the windows and screens. Mayne sat slumped in his chair as the assembled master-work or words faded limply from his mind. Another summer in Tokyo, he moaned to himself for the hundredth time that day, another month or more of this to endure. I may as well be stretched out on a bed of nails.

His hair hung over his forehead in sticky wet strands. Every time he shifted his position on the chair his underpants made a moist sucking sound. The words on the sheet of paper in the typewriter stared out obscenely at him. Hopeless, he thought, a publisher's nightmare, the whole thing. He wrenched the sheet of paper from the platten and tossed it into the waste basket.

Upstairs the baby began to cry and the mother's footsteps bounced quickly over the tatami. "That does it," he muttered, and he went into the bathroom and sank into the tubful of tepid water. In a few moments he was out again pulling on jeans and a fresh T-shirt. A long walk, he thought, a long, long walk to Shibuya, anything to escape his cell for a while and the chaos of stillborn words.

At the bottom of the steps he met Camus the cat coming out from under a parked car. The yellow, emaciated body seemed more like a discarded carcase than a living entity but in the moment of contact the spirit

94

that powered the eyes was unmistakable. As the cat leapt off up the steps Mayne thought: survival, that cat has lived forever and will go on living forever.

At the top of the side street Mayne turned from the plaza and set off in the direction of Shibuya. One by one he passed in memory the row of little shops he had once known: the pottery shop, fish market, greengrocer, pastry cook, the Chinese cafe, chicken soup, watchmaker, sushi restaurant, clothing seller, sake shop and all the other little shops and booths which seemed in memory to have sold everything the earth produced.

From behind the gilt and plateglass fronts of the merchants, coffee bars, real estate agents, western restaurants and fast food outlets, the voices of the past called to him. The cries of the shop keepers, door-framed, smiling, were vibrant with goodwill. Passing clearly and slowly in recollection, they were like old prints in a gallery denying the superimposed presence. Where are they now, Mayne thought, the fat fishmonger with the rogue's eye, the shy little lady in the pottery shop, the chicken man with the magician's hands . . .? One after the other they went so fast, in retrospect.

Interspersed in the gilt and glitter of the new facade slot machines grinned like psychotic robots dispensing canned beer, pies, condoms, sandwiches, cartons of cooked rice and cigarettes. Then the supermarket loomed, a glass and plastic palace sucking its thronging subjects in and spilling them out again like the balls from a pachinko machine.

Mayne stopped by a crossing and pressed the button. An old kimono-clad lady, gripping a power pole, turned her face to him. The eyes were naked slits of fear and confusion. In its frail cavity the lower lip trembled like a little girl about to burst into tears. The old lady motioned to the sea of traffic. In a voice surprisingly young and clear she murmured, "Excuse me, but even when the light tells me, I am afraid to cross."

Mayne extended his arm like a wing. The old lady took it with a gracious smile and when the lights changed they

95

walked slowly across the street. On the other side she bowed gratefully, murmuring her thanks, and was soon lost, wraith-like, in the surge of people on the pavement.

Mayne started down a stretch of narrow road, his walking space a metre of asphalt hemmed by a white line. The traffic sped past billowing dust and squeezing him now and then against walls and fences. New high-rise complexes and buildings under construction speared the hazed sky. Bulldozers coughed, churning the earth. Here and there in vacant lots the last traces of little old houses remained: door and window frames, torn screens, broken tiles and stacks of planking.

In the entrances and windows of the apartment buildings there were few signs of life. Each time I pass, Mayne thought, there are more buildings but the evidence of people is less. It was as if the latest neutron bomb had been detonated, eliminating the occupants but leaving the buildings intact. There were no children playing, no other feet on his wafer of asphalt.

The road turned from the residential district, twisted its way through a maze of office blocks and petered out at last in the main street of Shibuya. Overlaying the mechanical movements of his body as Mayne joined the avalanche of people on the sidewalk he had the strong impression of a hundred past occasions, all identical, the same puppet legs swinging before him, columns of eyes forming and reforming like soldiers on parade, a sea of voices spraying inaudible words.

Mayne mounted the steps of an elevated crossing and selected one of the walkways from the web suspended above the traffic. The foot-thudding deck swayed like a ship in a swell. Half-way across he stopped and leaned over the wooden railing. A two-way Amazon of traffic flowed beneath him. Its awesome gases and appetites channelled his mind to the sea and beyond it to the distant sources of energy that powered the flow. While the traffic roared and people scurried all about him he was touched by feelings of frailty and deep uncertainty as if while he looked down everything would come to a sudden stop. He turned slowly from the rail.

Continuing his circuit of the web, Mayne viewed the grandstand of department stores and commercial complexes that were his horizon. There was too much bulk and variety for specific focus. Bigger is better, brighter, bolder the buildings said. Enter and lose your mind in us. Fleetingly his eye caught the entrance of a small department store which he had once entered unsuspecting in the early days of the energy crisis and found himself struggling in the middle of a toilet paper panic-buying riot. How well he recalled the desperate looks on the shoppers' faces as he battled his way to the street door.

Mayne came down in Hachiko square and made his way slowly past the statue of the dog eternally waiting on its pedestal for the loved human who never came back. On the fringe of the crowd around the fountain he paused, caught up in the aura and frenzy of anticipation. He thought of Harumi magnifying in the sunlight, hurrying toward him . . . if only . . . their next meeting seemed light years away.

A figure in a red shirt in the centre of the crowd took Mayne's attention. The head was tossing, the body jigging and the lips emitting nervous puffs of smoke. Mayne moved forward and touched the red shoulder. The face turned, momentarily ecstatic, then confused. "Ha," Kato exclaimed at last, "so it's you. Well . . . ."

There was a glass-fronted coffee bar in the station building just beyond the dog. As they moved involuntarily toward the coffee bar Mayne said, "By the look of you I guess you would have been standing there for an hour or so. I know that feeling well."

"Two and a half hours exactly," Kato said. "She was very charming. We met at a bar in Shinjuku last Saturday night. When she promised she would come her eyes were so, how do you say in English . . . eloquent. I could almost read the good intentions like big letter words printed in her mind."

They perched on tiny chairs at a tiny table and a

97

waitress rushed to serve their iced orange juice. People surged in and out constantly like flocks of hungry sparrows. Some darted in from the crowd around the fountain and the dog, gulped their needs and hurried out again to resume the vigil. Under the floor, train wheels screeched like far away owls. Mayne said, "When did you first realize she would not turn up?"

The letdown in Kato's eyes was infused with moments of anger. In spite of the obvious distress his face was splendidly alert, the well fleshed mouth bright and mobile as if annointed with a cosmetic. "In the first few moments after I arrived I knew she would not come. I kept looking at the time and telling myself any moment now I would see her face coming from the station."

"Yes," Mayne said, "It is an old familiar sensation. No matter what you feel deep inside you just keep on standing, hoping and hoping."

They're all alike, Michiko was thinking, tall, short, thin, fat, handsome, ugly, intelligent, foolish, inside they're all alike. Only one thing makes them pretend to need you. She was smiling at Yamamoto, the Shinjuku innkeeper, while her hand simulated the enjoyment of his upper thigh.

"Ten, fifteen years ago," Yamamoto said, "the late night trade was predictable." Behind the thick-lensed, horn-rimmed spectacles his eyes looked as if they were gazing from the inside of a fish tank. "Nervous young couples, a little drunk, the girl giggling and trying to hide her face. Lots of older salary men with their one night stands."

Sex, sex, sex, Michiko thought, it is a wonder the country doesn't sink into the sea under the weight of it. But she liked Yamamoto, who drank his double whiskies without fuss and spoke to her frankly almost as though she were a man. How clearly she could see his thin little body unobtrusive as a rubber plant in the dim corridors of his inn. "I thought scx was scx wherever it took place," she said. "What's different about the trade these days?"

Yamamoto held out his glass and waited while she filled it. "Nowadays," he said, "people are so dishonest, you don't even know if the person you are dealing with is a man or a woman." His face saddened. "The world is changing so fast, sometimes I feel quite lost."

Me too, she thought, and gave his thigh a genuine squeeze. Yamamoto never tried to touch her and seemed to expect only the minimum from her fingers. "You mean gay boys and transvestites and that kind. Is that a problem for you?"

"Yes," Yamamoto said, "and lesbians and people who look straight and are not. What I really mean, Michiko, is that these days everything is upside down and back to front." He bent to his drink then straightened again, his voice palpitant with nostalgia. "In the old days, especially on Friday and Saturday nights, I used to tiptoe through the corridors listening. Everywhere there was the sound of moaning and sighing and trilling like ancient palace music and the soft cries were as harmonious as cuckoos and doves in a temple garden at sunrise." His voice sank into meditative silence.

Michiko looked at Yamamoto round-eyed. "It sounds, ah, wonderful," she murmured. "I have never thought of so many people doing it at the same time together except at those honeymoon hotels, but I suppose they're soundproofed. The changes of the present time must be quite shocking for you." She shot a glance at the booth where Akiko was purring with a merchant from Osaka then took a swift draft from her whisky glass.

"The other night," Yamamoto said, "a most handsome couple came to my inn. He was tall, a man of the world, with the physique of a promising weightlifter, she slim and pretty and as radiant as a bride. In fact they were more like a honeymoon couple than two people who had met only a short while ago in a bar. I was so happy to book them in. It was like the old days again." His face grew sad once more. "I had only been sitting at my desk for a few minutes when the first screams and angry shouts

99

began."

Michiko, for some oblique reason, had begun to think of Ishibashi. He would not be free to visit her again for another night or so. How could I miss such a thing, she thought, such a great big mass of a man. But she did miss him, she confessed, and she dreaded the thought of the long dark hours alone. To Yamamoto she said, "What happened, was there a fight or something?"

"A fight," Yamamoto exclaimed, "it was a raging battle. I opened the door with my pass key and there they were, striking at each other and hurling that word back and forth, cheat, cheat, cheat. Their clothes were all over the floor and when they turned to me I thought at last the new world must have driven me mad." He paused while Michiko raised his glass to his lips.

"Big handsome man was now most large womanly woman." Yamamoto formed a ' gross ovaloid shape between his extended forefingers and thumbs. "Radiant lady was a very thin angry little man." He gave an explicit drooping sign with his little finger. "Little man was so upset he rushed off without his panties or falsies and large lady left her padded jockstrap behind."

It could have been the whisky but Michiko was convinced there were tears in Yamamoto's eyes. She lit cigarettes for them both and carressed his thigh warmly. "Please don't let it trouble you too much. You must take good care of your health you know."

Yamamoto's head had begun to nod as though in agreement with an insistent inner voice. "Then there's the beds full of lubricants, creams and body oil and all the falsies and dildos and knicknacks they leave behind. The way this world is moving now soon there won't be any straights on earth. Really Michiko, frankly speaking it frightens me."

Slightly drunk now Yamamoto had begun to look old and frail. That's not what frightens me, Michiko thought, I'm just terrified of being alone. Again, the thought of Ishibashi flickered across her mind. How odd life was. The coarse voice and heavy flesh that had once only wounded her was now like a drug to help her sleep, to give her pleasure, and to cling to as the reality of day dawned in her little room. "Often," she said, "I hear people talking about straight people and those who are not straight. In your experience what is a straight person Yamamoto-san?"

Yamamoto's voice was priest-like in its retrospection. "I no longer know. There is a revolution going on. When it is finished the old roles of man and woman may have vanished for ever. Sometimes I feel like a foreigner lost in an alien language and culture. Soon I will sell the inn and retire to my son's peach orchard near Kofu. There I can sit in the sun with my old dreams and watch the growth of my grandchildren." He had begun to fumble with his wallet.

When Yamamoto's bill was paid Michiko guided him up the stairs and helped him into a taxi. As the gap between herself and the taxi lengthened she was struck with the thought that she would never see the innkeeper again. It was a rare premonition in her dealings with the clients of the White Bear and it troubled her.

On her way back through the bar still distracted with thoughts of Yamamoto she came face to face with Akiko. The smile in Akiko's eyes was exquisitely icy. "Well," the birdlike voice began, "is everything all right with you Michiko? Just a few moments ago I said to myself, wasn't there a little thing you had to tell Michiko? And here you are."

"What is it?" Michiko said, instantly apprehensive. "Was everything in order tonight?"

"Perfectly, I just forgot to mention a little discussion I had with Ishibashi when he was here the other night." The rose petal lips were quivering with fine intentions. "It seems you will be having a night off from the White Bear some time soon."

"Excuse me," Michiko said in some confusion, "but I cannot quite understand, a night off from here, from the White Bear?"

"An important friend of the syndicate is shortly to visit

Tokyo. The syndicate requested Ishibashi to find someone to entertain this very important guest and Ishibashi suggested you." The chill eyes latched briefly into a glow of inner satisfaction. "I agree with Ishibashi." She smiled. "In this matter he has excellent taste. You will get your instructions later. That is all."

Michiko went throught the mechanical processes of cleaning up with her mind in a turmoil. Once she caught the shock image of her face in the bar mirror, the mouth tight as if sealed against laughter and good thoughts, the eyes weary and hardened somehow. My image, my face, the little girl who came to Tokyo and grew up so fast.

Later she shared an illicit whisky with Mutsumi and was able to laugh when Mutsumi described how she had got her hair caught in an amorous client's zip. But try as she might she could not keep her thoughts from the future. She wanted Ishibashi and she needed reassurance and she could not help thinking of the innkeeper's words and the glow of satisfaction in Akiko's eyes.

How could you be so fond of someone for such a long time and then all of sudden see them with brand new eyes. Was this inevitable, Harumi pondered, in friendship and in love, seeping familiarity leading to boredom and even distaste? Dear Keiko, so close yet becoming so remote now. It would do no good no matter how she tried to impart her changed feelings. Keiko would only fly into a rage and blame Richard Mayne for wrecking their relationship.

They were lying on their backs on the tatami in Harumi's bedroom, their heads resting on cushions. The sky was darkening, easing the heat of the day from their unclad limbs. The dying strains of a Mozart violin piece were melting into the twilight fretfulness of the city, the screech and clatter of trains, the muffled barking of dogs, a child's wailing cry, a ball hitting a wall and the wasp-like buzzing of motorcycles over the traffic's dull roar.

Keiko said, "Remember those first days after we met at

102

university how bright everything was, shopping for all those things we couldn't afford in the department stores, the fabulous food we found in those quaint little out of the way cafes and the first night together in Shinjuku. How many new tastes and smells and sights we discovered." She clasped Harumi's hand. "Everything stood out so sharp and clear and in such vivid colour. It was always like the fresh sparkle after rain.

"Often when I was sitting in my room thinking, where is Harumi now, what is she doing? the telephone would ring and suddenly your voice would be coming to me. That was the magic of Tokyo in those days. It scared me sometimes. Now even in summer the city is grey, the colours have all faded. Why?"

Harumi was thinking. He is teaching now at his table, his mind is tired and he is repeating, "The rapid rabbit ran around the block at eleven o'clock." The student cannot hear him. Patiently he begins again . . . . She said, "Because other summers have passed and we are older. The city is much the same, only we are changing."

"Have we really changed so much?" Keiko's voice was rising. "I certainly don't think I am much different these days, especially in certain ways."

His face is bent, shielding his frustration and fatigue from his student. Now he is smiling, yes, yes . . . he can see me . . . at me. But I must try to centre my mind on Keiko, I must or my thoughts of him will show. Harumi turned her face to Keiko and smiled. "Of course I remember the happy times, the dreams of our future, how we would travel together to foreign countries then return to Japan and settle down. Remember the pamphlets — how many there were — we used to dream over, on such fabulous places as the Swiss Alps, the Costa Brava and the Grand Canyon. How those travel agents must have tired of us."

"Then we would find our unique Japanese husbands, gentle poets or teachers. We did not mind the profession so much as long as they were gentle, and we would live happily ever after." Keiko's mouth, Harumi was pleased

103

to see, was softening, her eyes lightening.

"Yes, and on our wedding night we could pretend to be virgins so we could laugh at every intimate detail of the hoax when the honeymoon was over." As the nostalgic chuckles passed away Keiko went on: "But seriously, Haru-chan, tonight I wish to discuss our future — yours and mine."

Now it is coming, Harumi thought, and she resigned herself to the predictable theme. Through the fingers interlocking her own she felt the tension mounting. The tatami was now like cool, smooth skin on her skin. Was he white all over, the unseen parts? She shivered. Be careful, she will see . . . .

"I will speak frankly. There is nothing to hide." Keiko had drawn closer. "First it is a matter of simple economics that those who live alone pay more than those who live together. You know Haru-chan how the spiral of food and power charges is getting beyond us now. We know each other so well. Then why should not we live together and pool our resources?"

Harumi could feel the subtle overture of Keiko's toes feathering her instep. Just stay calm and relaxed and in agreement and all will be well, she told herself. "It is commonsense, Keiko, I know we have talked about it in the past."

"Yes, and as matters are shaping, for women who live like us these days, it is also a matter of survival." She gave a brief sardonic laugh. "Those starry eyes we brought to Tokyo saw husbands waiting everywhere. But what did those blind bridegrooms think of us? One night stands for their leaping little egos and virgin slaves as brides." She disengaged her hand and curved it unselfconsciously on Harumi's breast. "If we were to live together, Haru-chan, more important than economics, survival even, there would be companionship and love."

In the faint neon glow infiltrating the room Keiko's eyes were now out of reach but Harumi was increasingly aware of the breath quickening on her shoulder and the hand carressing slowly downward from her breast. She lay still, neither angry nor afraid, feeling the intensity of Keiko's need. At last she murmured, "I understand fully, Keiko, of course it makes commonsense to share."

Keiko's voice was becoming uneven. "Think of the freedom. Only ourselves. No husbands to light cigarettes and baths for and no babies to wash. And no contraception or abortion to make our minds anxious. Oh Haru-chan, can you imagine, we could wake to the sunrise together every morning."

As the arm encircled her and the hand moved downward Harumi thought, this urgent, hard-breathing Keiko whose fingers want to excite music from me like plucking the strings of the koto . . . this stranger-friend Keiko, if only she could open my mind now and perceive his clarity she would hate me forever.

"We could take our trip at last. All those fabulous overseas places we used to talk about." Her lips moved in the hollow of Harumi's neck. The words were rapid, indistinct. "And in Tokyo, I am sure you know, these days there are lots of places, bars, coffee bars and clubs for people like us where we could just be ourselves. Oh Haru-chan you excite me, you know what I'm trying to say. There, yes, like that, please, please let me love you Haru-chan . . . ." The telephone rang.

Harumi disengaged herself, sprang to her feet and went swiftly to the vestibule. She faced the street door. The receiver trembled in her hand. "I had to call. I hope it's not too late. I felt somehow you were wanting to hear me."

With some difficulty she steadied herself and got her voice as low as possible. "No, it's not too late, I knew you would call. It's wonderful to hear your voice. It's like magic. I was just thinking about you a moment ago." Her hand, as if of its own will, warmed to the inner part of her thighs. She was amazed at the deep sensation of readiness for him and was afraid her voice would betray her. "This place is in darkness," she murmured. "Can you imagine how I am feeling?"

Mayne chuckled. "Would you believe it if I said I could

actually see you. Well, believe it or not, right at this moment I feel certain I can. In fact I've seen nothing else but the image of Harumi all day. You can't imagine what you're doing to the lights in this mind of mine."

There was no sound from Keiko. Surely she had not fallen asleep. "Never mind my teacher, I am, how do you say, counting the hours till my next lesson. Your student will come to your door as usual just as the clock is striking. Now I must say good-night and try to sleep."

He was murmuring, "Good night, sleep well Harumi," and the handpiece was dropping to its cradle as Keiko silently entered the room. She moved past Harumi without a word and put on her shoes in the vestibule.

Harumi stood motionless, not knowing if she should switch on the light. Then Keiko's voice came, flat calm in the darkness. "I never wish to see you again. Please erase my name and my memory from your mind." The door clicked softly behind her.

On the table, beside the open diary, there was a half-full glass of whisky and the ever-ready Japanese-English dictionary. Noguchi sat relaxedly back on his heels alternately sipping whisky and going through the pages of the diary. Behind him, over the creaking and sighing of the house he could hear the steady rhythm of his sons' breathing. From beyond the screens, in the room in front where his wife lay, there was the high-strung silence of reproach.

Noguchi was thinking about Richard Mayne. He would not say goodbye to him. Their relationship would end like the snapping shut of a book. But the book could always be opened again and browsed through at any time. The influence of Mayne the teacher was the strongest force in the life of his mind; it would never die. How much of the life and spirit of Mayne these pages contained.

Noguchi turned the page and stopped at the familiar heading, Misconceptions Held by the Foreigners Before Coming to Japan. "The Japanese are scrupulously honest,

106

friendly to foreigners and well mannered. If a Japanese stops you in Ginza and says, 'May I speak English with you?' he does so because he thinks your race and culture is superior to his own. With foreigners Japanese will not discuss the Pacific war, family intimacies and problems, sexuality, religion or Japanese politics. The Japanese woman is wholly devoted to the pleasure and welfare of her husband-lover. Marriages between white Caucasian males and Japanese females are the most stable and harmonious of any inter-racial union. The Japanese husband is supreme master in his own home." Noguchi smiled at this heavily underscored entry and came to his footnote.

"Mayne introduced to me a new word today, hogwash. This word, he said, applies to all the generalisations above. Mayne assured me that the list of misconceptions as quoted above is endless. The Japanese, he told me, are only all or any of the above if they travel overseas in large tour groups." On the opposite page, beneath the heading, Japanese Misconceptions of the White Caucasian, Noguchi read: "English teachers are round and fat with pink faces and they are very jolly. Using a loud, frank voice you can say anything you wish to a foreigner. They will only laugh good naturedly. All white Caucasians living in Tokyo are from the United States of America. The erect white Caucasian penis is two centimetres longer than the erect Japanese penis. All Americans are frank and generous and always wear casual clothes. No white Caucasian ever speaks understandable Japanese.

"Every white Caucasian on earth is a practising Christian. The one desire of young white Caucasian females in Japan is to be constantly touched on trains and pursued by amorous Japanese males. No white Caucasian is ever to be trusted. Auld Lang Syne is not of Scots origin but was in fact composed by Watanabe Yukio in Japan in October 1912 . . . ."

How they had laughed, shouted and agonised in their discussions, Noguchi mused. The territory of the foreigner was a brand new world to him. What oblique inspiration,

107

he wondered, had driven him in the first place to seek contact with a person of another race. Was it because he had given up hope of meaningful communication with his own people? The diary perhaps was the answer.

As he slowly turned the pages threading his existence Noguchi said, "Haa," and "So indeed," and smiled and crinkled his toes in embarrassment. At times he stopped, listening to the rhythm of his sons in sleep and the elastic silence on the other side of the house. He saw the diary on the table replete with the word symbols of his creation and perceived simultaneously from outside himself the man of his flesh, Noguchi at the table. I exist, I am, the inner cry rang again and again. I am Noguchi . . . .

For just a moment longer the force of insight held him. When it had passed his hand returned to the pages and the words began to come to life once more. The entries echoed through the family home, primary school, high school, the first company dormitory, the army and the war. How dim and distant now and utterly insane, that war.

Out of the shadows the memory of that last day came: the blazing sun, the hot white sand of the southern Kyushu beach, the sparkling sea. In the azure blue sky there was neither ash nor breath of Hiroshima or Nagasaki. Noguchi's eyes drew the words from the page.

"The night of the end-of-war disbanding party was not without trouble. At that time, apart from the local villagers, there were three groups: our wireless telegraph squad, a small naval group who were building a shelter for a suicide attack boat, and a squad of Koreans attached to the navy who were also working on the construction of the suicide boat shelter.

"At the announcement of the ending of the war the group of Koreans held celebrations in their hut all night. From that moment the Koreans spoke no Japanese and sang their own national song. Among so many in low spirits, only they were rejoicing.

"But trouble broke out between our fellows and the navy group. After the disbanding party M., a private first

108

class, visited a man who was the master of a small mine. By chance the mine master was drinking sake with the navy sergeant. M. disturbed their conversation. At once a dispute began between M. and the navy sergeant. M. threw his wine glass at the navy sergeant and cut his brow deeply. Then he threw another glass at the lamp, put out the light and escaped. He was a stirrer of trouble.

"I heard of this trouble when I was awakened on the party floor after a night of heavy drinking. Anticipating trouble from the navy I ordered M. to get away at once and gave him some food. Then I altered our departure time from the village to earlier that morning.

"In the morning very early when we were about to depart the navy sergeant and his fellows came to us. The navy sergeant demanded 200 yen and the assailant but I refused his demands. Suddenly he gave me a heavy blow and knocked me down. In the presence of the navy men, the villagers and my fellows the navy sergeant said to me, "I have been eating the navy rations for 20 years. You are a fool." I had never had any experience of being struck by a person. I kept quiet barely.

"The villagers, navy men and my squad fellows attending this scene surrounded us at a distance. I stood up, drew my Japanese sword and addressed my squad. "Fall in all members." For the first time I noticed their strained faces, former customs officer, farmer, fisherman, carpenter, policeman and so on as if they were preparing to attack the navy.

"I was aware suddenly that I had been prepared for death. I raised my sword. 'All members dismiss,' I said, 'the war is over.' "

Recollection of that moment flooded back: the murmur of the sea, the stark eyes of his comrades, the stinging pain in his cheek. Noguchi sighed. It was the culmination of his loneness, the birth of a new isolation. He had kept the moment locked away for an age. Its liberation came one night with Richard Mayne over pot after pot of sake in a chicken liver cafe. And that night, Noguchi knew well,

109

marked the beginning of his own liberation.

"Bring it all out," Mayne had said, "the hurting, the shame and the laughter. Let the mind study it slowly and thoughtfully like the prints in an old album. Then write it down, every word. After a while it will fade and die like the ink."

A cough broke the silence of the inner room. Its irritated inflexion was clear. "Leave your diary and your ancient dreams my now-and-then husband and get yourself to bed." Noguchi drained his glass and shut the diary.

"There was no time," Ishibashi said, "I had much business to attend." He was lying back in the bed, a whisky-water in his hand. "I told you many times. I will come when I can. But you cannot expect me."

Michiko read the impatience in his tone. It was after 3.30am and the desire for sleep clashed with the joy at not being alone. She sat on the tatami in the lee of Ishibashi's bare chest. He does not need any words. How frankly, how separately, his need, the need of a man arises. Softly she said, "Yes, you have been very busy. I understand. Please excuse me."

The questions that had been churning in her mind for days now clamoured for expression. A thousand times she had asked the ceiling, the walls, the toilet, the bath, but she had to wait for the right moment to put them to Ishibashi. She leaned over the bed and ran her hands up and down the twitching stem of his preoccupation. Delicately she cushioned it between her breasts then touched the tip against her nipples. Ishibashi groaned softly and began to move against her. Patience, she thought, yours, mine, the moment will come.

The words of a pop song sprang into her mind. "When I'm alone I see only your face, your face is the only love I know." She drew down her face and touched the springing staff to her neck, cheeks and eyes. Gently she squeezed open the tiny pink mouth and inserted the tip of her tongue. "My room is warm and waiting," the song crooned, "my door lonely for your hand."

There was no taste, no trace of bitter wife, others. The bath had washed them all away . . . all? What a busy man he was, always in the bars of Shinjuku on syndicate business. She took him into her mouth, eager, darting, tracing the smooth sculptured roundness with lips and tongue. It filled her mouth driving out loneliness, the words of the song. Big man, I am drunk with you, my weariness is gone.

He grunted, twining his fingers in her hair, holding her fast to the peak of his rhythm. She took him avidly, now, now, one hand cupping, squeezing below. She sucked. The fingers in her hair relaxed, the pulses in her mouth died. She let him out slowly, licking. At last she laid him damp, diminished on the bed of pubic hair.

Michiko lit cigarettes, filled the glasses and sat close again. Ishibashi's eyes were half shut, the heavy breathing slowly returning to normal. She looked at him obliquely, absorbing each detail. His face is rounder, fatter, his stomach bigger. He looks like a worn out sumo wrestler and a sleepy little boy. What is he thinking now? Do I ever know, ever? In a low, matter-of-fact voice she said, "Akiko spoke to me. She said I would have a night off soon from the White Bear. There is an important person to entertain. You had discussed this matter with her."

Ishibashi opened his eyes and glanced briefly at her. "Yes, well, it is not such a very important matter to discuss now. A special guest is coming. He has friends in high places, but your part is small. You will see to his entertainment for one night, that is all."

She plucked up courage, shooting the words out before they could be stopped. "Is this what you wish . . . that I spend a night entertaining this man?" She glanced directly at Ishibashi.

"You entertain men every night — why should this be different?" Ishibashi's eyes followed a cloud of smoke drifting toward the ceiling.

"But that is at the White Bear, not with one man alone,

111

that is just . . . business."

"So is this — syndicate business and the syndicate has requested your services." He put his empty glass in her hand. "The syndicate, by the way, does not like questions."

There was no doubting the sting in his voice now. Michiko refilled both glasses and matched his swallow. It was like talking to a stone wall. She smiled bitterly to herself. But he is the only wall I know. Again she inflated her courage. "Then you are not displeased with me?"

A rare half smile toyed for a moment with Ishibashi's lips. "No, not when you are obedient. Now is my free time, my time for relaxing."

In the pensive silence that followed thought of the foreigner came inexplicably to Michiko's mind. She had seen him at his door that evening letting out a salary man student. He had looked across the courtyard at her and smiled as if he were her friend. How many walls has the English teacher got, she wondered and she was annoyed at herself for letting even thought of the man invade her mind.

Soon the sun would rise and the apartment would begin to bake. Once she had suggested to Ishibashi that they get up together and watch the sun rise one morning. He had looked at her as if she were in a manic state. "Where shall we go?" he demanded. "To the top of the Tokyo Tower? And what shall we see then, a pale egg frying in grey smoke?" After that she had not risked the intrusion of further suggestions. She simply waited and let the silences between them grow.

As she was about to lie beside him and give herself up to the weariness within her Ishibashi reached for her, guiding her to a position full length on top of him. His arms came around her buttocks and thighs. His touch, the heat of his flesh, recharged her. Yes, there, she implored silently, there, hold me, touch me. She moved lower, arching her thighs over his hips, delighting at the ease of penetration.

Her lips touched his cheek. His eyes were shut. If only I could let him see me now and he could draw my feeling into him, could suck me down through these eyes hot and alive, could swallow me and never let me out. She raised herself then let the head, the whole length, slowly in again.

"Iku, iku," Michiko heard the voice of the stranger cry. It startled her. "Iku, iku." My voice? Just for a moment his eyes opened. The pupils, dark as midnight, dilated. 'Iku, iku." She let herself in. "Iku, iku." Deeper. "Iku, iku." . . . Darkness.

Part 4

Mayne took the tray chinking with empty ceramics to the door and laid it outside on the flagstones. The blended fragrance of chow mein, cooked rice and sake lingered in the late evening air. He moved slowly inside again through the warm breezes stirred by the fan. He picked up a white envelope from under a book and went into the tatami room.

In the same green silk dress she had worn when they had first met Harumi was sitting on the tatami thinking, there is so much time, I feel as free as the silk around me. He moves so calmly. He is also thinking tonight there is time . . . .

As Mayne eased on to the tatami beside her she caught sight of the envelope in his hand. "Here," he said, "please take this, I can't use it now."

Recognising the envelope Harumi hesitated. "But it is my, aah, fee. I am your student, you are my teacher. It was our agreement." She took the envelope uncertainly then caught the good humour in Mayne's eyes. "Are you my teacher, really?"

He laughed. "Well, no, not now, not exactly. I knew when I first touched this envelope I would give it back to you one day." For a moment, with extraordinary clarity, the sensation of past images revived — the green dress and golden tatami, the slim olive fingers on the white envelope, the lovely receptive eyes . . . "I only wish to be your friend."

Harumi tucked the envelope out of sight in her handbag. "I did not expect such a thing. You are very kind." In her ears her response sounded inadequate, but she would buy him a gift, a special memento that would equal the sum of the tuition fee. "By the way," she said at last, "we have met a few times but hardly discussed each other's lives. Time just passes, how do you say, like an arrow."

"Yes it's true," he said. "I have lots of questions but when I am with you they just seem to vanish. I guess for me just being with you is knowing about you." He heard the unmistakable wail of Camus from the other end of the alley.

Harumi was thinking, what can I tell him of my life that is interesting. He has met so many like me before.

"My day to day existence is so commonplace," she said. "When it comes to my life I am at a loss for words."

"Please tell me about your mother. She must be lonely and perhaps a little anxious about you sometimes."

Harumi fended a desire to giggle. If only her mother's eyes could discover her now even her worst fears would be overshadowed. "These days my mother is very busy. She and my uncle Hiroshi take care of our family land in Fukushima. When I go back at New Year sometimes they are always talking about land and the latest price for this piece and that. My mother is very, a moment please," she checked her dictionary, ". . . traditional."

Beyond the rear door Mayne saw a grey tabby cat sidling up the alley. Then from the unseen Camus there was a deep tom-catting growl. As if frozen by command the tabby stopped just beyond the stoop. Mayne said, "I understand, you are in Tokyo now, she is there. Your lives are quite separate."

"Yes," Harumi nodded. "We were so close once. Now I feel we are in different worlds. We seem to have no common language any more." She was astonished at the ease

116

with which she was able to talk to Mayne and while the dialogue went on she was conscious of the hidden language, too subtle for word interpretation yet so explicit in the eyes. Impulsively she said, "But I am happy here."

There was a yowling, hissing commotion in the alley. Mayne was not surprised at last to see Camus settling blatantly on to the back of the tabby. As Harumi turned to look, Camus sank his mouth into the back of the tabby's neck and began to undulate sinuously on her, his indomitable yellow eyes staring fixedly into the room.

While Camus built up his snarling, thrusting tempo Mayne glanced at Harumi. "He is a terrible cat. He tries to embarrass us and to shame me. Please excuse the manners of my yellow friend."

"Never mind," she said laughing, "I think I have met such a cat before." Camus was too outrageously natural for her to be anything but amused. Viewing his act in another setting with another man perhaps, that could be different. The eyes would not see and the ears would not hear. Only the mind would acknowledge discomfort.

There was a sudden blaze of howling and hissing in the alley and a brief fountain of yellow and grey. Then silence. Mayne got up laughing and prepared drinks. When he had returned to his place on the tatami they clinked glasses. "To Camus and survival," he said. "To us," she echoed, smiling.

Mayne shut the alley door, drew the screens together and switched on the table lamp. They sat in silence sipping their drinks, intent on the new golden glow sheening the tatami. Harumi was wondering if she should try his name aloud. Richard, Richard — it sounded correct in her mind. Making the 'r' unmistakably clear she would say, Richard . . . shall we have a record?

Inside and out, as if they were the centre, the silence expanded around them. She was about to speak when she felt his hand on her arm. The look in his eyes stopped her like a bullet. For a moment longer the stillness hung. They sat gazing into each other, unable to move, waiting.

Then the glasses on the tray started to dance and

117

tinkle, the night light bowed and the screens began to chatter. Overhead the baby was crying and the mother beginning to bounce across the bouncing tatami. "It's a bad one," Mayne murmured, and they were in each other's arms rocking on the mats as the noise and shaking grew.

Harumi felt the undulations and the quakings of the earth and the shaking and the rocking of the building through the medium of Mayne's body. It is like shaking a peach tree heavy with ripe fruit, she thought. His neck, his chest, how pleasant he smells. Soon, when a certain point is reached, like a whisper the fruit will begin to fall. Then it will come tumbling down on top of us, around us. The climax is coming, I can feel it inside me. How slow and regular the beat of his heart — thumpa thump, thumpa thump, thumpa thump . . . .

Mayne whispered, "Now it is passing." And she felt his lips opening hers. Upstairs the baby was whimpering, the mother crooning. She felt his tongue, took it and gave her own. The undulations were passing into spasmodic tremors then minute palpitations like quivering skin. His mouth is warm, alcohol, unsweet, I love his tongue in me. Out in the streets the sounds of ambulances, police cars and fire engines were beginning.

With wayward fingers they helped each other undress. Steady, Mayne told himself as she came into his arms at last. Slow down. But he was breathless with excitement, bewildered by the immediacy of her perfection. He kissed her eyes, cheeks. You smell of fresh almonds. Words are hopeless, inadequate. This skin, this warmth, this curving velvet smoothness . . . stop my mouth, my words . . . .

"My teacher," she murmured into his neck. The all over intensity of feeling was almost choking her. She wanted to pleasure him, tickle him, occupy him in devious ways but she was too overcome by excitement to act. My teacher, my naked teacher, how deep his chest, how smooth and white his skin. In a distant space in her mind she was aware of the growing magnitude of his response. As they lay together it became unbelievably bigger and bigger in her mind.

"Shall I put on a record?" Mayne whispered, "Some Vivaldi, Mozart?" He wanted to expand time, to prolong and soften these moments. "Just for us?"

"Yes," she murmured, "please," and kept her eyes shut as he stood up. When the music had begun and he was standing above her again she opened her eyes. It was unbelievable and in a way so foreign and removed from them both. Instinctively she drew her thighs together. As he came down beside her she murmured weakly, "I saw, I can hardly believe."

Mayne laughed softly and lay a little apart from her. "Is it really so terrible? After all it's only a part of me, a very natural and important part." Secretly the little boy in him was delighted if not boastful; it was a pretty good performance he must admit.

In the pale lamp glow it stood out white as a lily. Harumi reached out a timid hand and clasped it. It palpitated hotly. Her hand in contrast looked like a small child's. "It looks foreign," she whispered, "strange, not like you at all. It, aaah, how do you say, fascinates me."

"I suppose in moments like this they are all different, foreign in their own way. We are so accustomed to clothes and masks. I hear though that Japanese men when properly stimulated can hold up twenty-kilo weights with theirs. But here, let me introduce you to this strange friend." They drew close again laughing softly, kissing, fondling one another.

Now, Harumi thought, I can wait no more. The tatami was moist warm on her back. She drew her thighs far back on either side of his chest and opened to him. As her hand reached to show him the way she whispered into the tickling hairs on his chest, "Too big, too big, please, I can't take it." And she began to struggle against him and herself. But in a few moments she found his body hard against her and was touching with wondering fingers their damp entwining pubic hair.

The strains of Vivaldi came in brief, poignant flashes. The tatami squeaked. Harumi's mind was wild with movement and the sensation of being so fully taken. He seemed to last forever, taking her from plateau to plateau,

119

closer and closer, until she felt at last the culmination of his energies in long hard spasms spending within her. They lay still, his cheek wet on her breasts, his breath returning.

In a few moments Harumi chided in a tiny child-like voice, "A while ago it was too big and hurtful to enter, now it is too weak and little to stay in. How quickly it changes its shape." She giggled. Then she caressed him and kissed him and felt with satisfaction his excitement flexing within her again.

"For us," Mayne whispered, "there is so much time I can scarcely believe it." He was idling his tongue on Harumi's nipple. The luxury of exhiliration still dazed him. He had gone so high and not come down and was already astonishingly erect once more. "There is time," he whispered, "for music and kisses and this . . . do you like it? . . . and that."

Noguchi took a piece of mackerel and carried it on his chopsticks to his mouth. He liked the piquant taste of the fish and the assorted aromas of the table — boiled rice, pickled cabbage, clear soup and green tea. Already his sons had left for school, leaping through the door without a backward glance and quarrelling high spiritedly over baseball as their voices faded down the road. Breakfast for Noguchi's wife and sons was white bread toast and coffee with a touch of laughter for his adherence to tradition.

His wife was sweeping, grumbling softly in another room. She was anxious for him to leave her alone so she could chastise every centimetre of space, drive out dirt and dust and smells and have at last the whole sterilised domain to herself. Then and only then she could think about what had to be done and undone and television could be reborn. Without him and with the opiate of television she could be herself until her sons came home. Noguchi slurped his clear soup appreciatively and smiled to himself.

As was often his custom over breakfast his mind turned

to Mayne. His teacher would be waking, cursing the heat, the sluggishness of his thoughts and the stubbornness of the typewriter waiting on the table. He would sweat and bathe and sweat again and feel the ceiling bearing down on him and he would swear to himself that this was his last summer in Tokyo, especially after last night's rather severe earthquake. Poor Mayne, my teacher, he has taught me so much, more than any man and like every man he has so much to learn.

Noguchi took some rice and washed it down with green tea. With immense satisfaction and consummate ease he conjured up the image of his president at that moment, the tiny skull drawn taught with pain and remorse. At 10am there was a directors' meeting requiring papers to be put in order and things to be said correctly, and he the president, the superhuman, had yet another Ginza hangover. And what was worse, his ulcer was playing up again, errupting in the most inappropriate moments like Sakura-jima in heat. Noguchi delicately uplifted the last piece of mackerel and smiled again.

The sweeping and grumbling was gaining momentum. Be gone, the angry broom was complaining, your place is elsewhere. If only she knew . . . had the slightest inkling . . . if only he and she could run wires into each other's minds and exchange the correct signals. When, in all the intimacies of a lifetime together, had they last communicated? Had they ever communicated their real thoughts? Still, to either of them no blame could be apportioned. It was simply the gap between the infinite world of the mind and the tedious irrelevance of the human body.

Noguchi poured green tea and thought of his sons, the joy of their birth, their early childhood. What strange quirk of the imagination had induced him to believe that the filial bond would go on forever. The world of the sons was a foreign country to the father, the world of the father an extra-terrestrial body to the sons. Neither boy had looked into his eyes for years. He drained his teacup. Never mind, their education and financial security would continue; a long while ago, together with their mother's

121

welfare, he had begun to take care of that.

As Noguchi stood in the vestibule jiggling his shoes into position his wife appeared. She picked up his briefcase and handed it to him smiling through clenched teeth. If she had noticed that the briefcase was unduly heavy she gave no sign. It was only when he came home and she felt the weight of a bottle of whisky in it that she let her feelings be known. Now he thought of all his treasures lying snugly inside — Herman Hesse, Basho, his sub-soul, the new book on mountain herbs and plants, and the other precious items he had transferred from his desk drawer at the office. Through the grip of the briefcase he felt the solid comforting weight.

His wife's farewell came out at last with the vitality of a spent breath. They turned from each other and he took the narrow road to the station. Passing the little houses, dollshouse apartment blocks and contrasting high-rise complexes his eyes co-ordinated without effort the everyday details of normality. All is well, as yesterday, the day before and the day before that and functioning exactly on schedule. At intersections and the points where lanes and footpaths fed, as if yesterday or the day before in the same split second, the identical people stepped precisely into time and joined the throng toward the station. There were no greetings, smiles, whistles or songs but by the time the centre of the town was reached the streets were flooded with people.

Outside the station Noguchi stood in line in front of the battery of hard-pressed ticket-selling machines. When it was his turn he inserted the coin, extracted his ticket and moved on. From here, he thought, there is no need for eyes or a brain. The mass would take him like a conveyor belt through the ticket barrier and up the steps to his platform. Soon he would be swept mindless into a carriage and trapped there until he was swept out again at Shinjuku. There was nothing to feel except sweating, unidentifiable flesh, nothing about this part of the journey to be remembered.

Michiko passed between the spinning glass doors and

entered the foyer of the new world. For a moment she stood on the thick red carpet allowing her senses to adjust to the strange scene expanding around her. The lobby was like a great ballroom on television, seething with colour, noise and people, stretching beyond the imagination. The fluttering in her abdomen and the constriction in her throat signalled her to leave, run back into the twilight, jump into a taxi and with kamikaze speed return to the known. All afternoon, resting, bathing, dressing, she had been troubled by the approach of this moment. It was too late now to turn back.

On legs that seemed not to belong to her she made her way through the crowd to the nest of grey vinyl armchairs flanking the elevators. She sat down, crossed her thighs and smoothed the black skirt down over her legs. From where she sat she was able to take in most reaches of the lobby. It seemed larger now, even less real than the first impression by the door. She lit a cigarette and watched the smoke wreathing toward other smoke. The clock above the elevators told her she was five minutes early.

Japanese hostesses in light gold kimonos bustled past not looking at her but saying with their eyes: take care, we are watching, this place is not for you. Foreign tour groups were disbanding, clucking around their guides like chicks around the mother hen. A man in a white cloth cap, who looked as if his blue shirt had been stuffed with a mountain of plastic foam, called in a loud voice across the lobby, "Hey Charlie, how come you missed out on our tour. We went right through a genuine Jap home."

The aroma of cigar smoke, deodorants, liquor and expensive perfumes stifled the conditioned air. Along the far wall neon signs glowed — hamburgers, massage, beauty parlour, cocktails, souvenirs . . . .From the babble of foreign voices Michiko could not isolate a single word. She puffed her cigarette and felt the tension knotting within her.

A young man in a midnight blue suit stepped from an elevator, glanced at the nest of chairs then approached her. "Are you Michiko? . . . Well, it is good, I am Sadao. Shall we go upstairs?"

123

In the rocketing elevator Sadao said, "Our guest has had a very busy day. Now he is taking a shower." He glanced at her sidelong and gave a knowing smile. "I have instructions to leave as soon as he appears."

A gangster's apprentice, Michiko thought. She knew the young man's type well; there were many such Sadaos employed to do the less pleasant tasks of Ishibashi's syndicate. "Who is this guest?" she said to the smooth, uncaring face as the elevator door slid open.

The eyes were hooded. "A very special guest. He has friends in the highest places. The syndicate is anxious to take good care of him." They had begun to walk down a long carpeted corridor.

Sadao opened a door and ushered her inside. The room was large and windowless with steel-grey walls and a light green carpet. There were two grey vinyl armchairs and a sumptuous cream settee. In front of the settee a coffee table was stacked with liquor, ice and glasses, plates of sandwiches and bowls of colourful salad. Michiko viewed the food with disdain but noted the bottle of Black Label. Unlike the White Bear the whisky would be true to label. Only the best, she thought, for people with friends in high places and those who entertain them.

She sat on the settee facing the switched off television set and a large refrigerator in a corner. On the wall above the television there was a woodblock print of a courtesan. The face was as round as a peach, black lacquered spikes of hair hung over the forehead, the eyebrows arched like ravens' wings and there was a toothpick rackishly between the lips. The ageless face looked down wickedly at Michiko and said: I know why you are here beautiful one. Michiko drew her eyes quickly from the familiar face.

She accepted a whisky-ice from Sadao, gratified by its generous size. Its taste, strong and mellow, bolstered her briefly. But the whisky could not dispel her mounting unease or the awareness of the faint sound of water falling in an adjoining room. Sadao stood by the door ready to leave. He did not speak to her now. She lit a cigarette. If only there were windows, glimpses of the twilit city, something everyday and tangible to link the past with

124

now. Even sight of the White Bear would be welcome.

A door clicked. Sadao spoke halting words she could not understand then he spoke to her in Japanese and she stood up. "This is Ivory-san. He says you may call him Carl." The outer door shut and Sadao was gone.

Michiko stood staring, holding her cigarette, twining her fingers in the strap of her handbag. The man was big, much bigger even than Ishibashi. There was a moist smile on his full pink lips. He had thinning blond hair and there were deep pouches under his eyes and grooves around the corners of his mouth. But it was his eyes, pale blue and unwavering, that struck her. They had the same chilling disregard as Akiko's eyes. He looked at her, slowly, directly, all over and said at last, "Well, Michiko, I'm sure we'll have a fine time together. This is my last night." She recognised only "Michiko", strangely pronounced.

A foreigner? . . . A foreigner? Shock and fear were being overtaken now by outrage. She saw Akiko's flower face petalled into smiles, heard Ishibashi's booming laugh. A foreigner and Michiko? Can you see it? Can you imagine?

The red silk dressing gown the man wore was half open exposing the pink rise of his over large belly. There was a pungent meaty smell in Michiko's nostrils; she had picked it up faintly on entering the room. They sat down together on the settee. She put out her cigarette.

The man half filled a glass with whisky and put in some ice. His hand trembled slightly. As if by slow patient utterance his words would be magically understood he began painstakingly, "My name is Carl. I come from Chicago in the United States. I am in the hotel business." He looked over the top of his glass, smiling, his eyes invading her like a hand groping in flesh. "This trip has been very busy. Now I am relaxing. I want a good time. Do you understand?"

Understanding nothing but what his eyes told her Michiko shook her head. His thigh had begun to overlap her with hot, sickening pressure. She drained her glass and refilled it, her mind in a daze. The man pointed to

125

her and to himself, then he linked his hands under his cheek and dropped his head. Ever so slowly, softly, he said, "I have had a busy day. I want to go to bed, with you. Understand?"

The dressing gown had slipped wide open. The man wore nothing underneath. Michiko thought distractedly, why does he make his childish signs when the language of that part is so plain? Fear was setting in. There was no outlet, no way to cope with the situation. She looked up at the woodblock print; the wicked eyes said, Yes, I know why you are here, beautiful one. Now use your ancient remedy on him. After all he is just another man.

The man moved closer and put his hand on Michiko's thigh. He talked faster now. "I've no time for tactics, God dammit, I want you, can't you see that?" There was a fixed smile on his lips that was not reflected in his eyes. "Carl Ivory gets what he wants, straight up and down or sideways. It's all the same to me. Understand?"

The big pink hands were strong. There was no more pretence. She lay wedged into the corner of the settee as he fought to lay bare her skin. He intruded his mouth wetly, thrusting his face against her. She bit his lip, drawing blood. He drew back his head, still smiling.

Quickly she stood up, reached for the whisky bottle and crashed it down on his head with all her strength. The bottle broke, showering the settee with whisky and splinters of glass. The man slumped sideways. Michiko dropped the bottle neck on to the carpet, picked up her bag and went to the door. She did not look back.

Since her moments upstairs time seemed to have stood still in the lobby. She passed between the tour groups and the hostesses amid the heavy call and burr of voices. Her pantytights were torn; that did not matter, her skirt was long enough and there was no blood on her clothes. She moved swiftly feeling strangely light and free. There was little time and there was time infinite now, beyond calculation.

By the darkening kerb a taxi was waiting. She sank on to the seat covers. The kamikaze driver nodded and smiled and they began to move. She laid back her head, her eyes wide. Soon, it seemed, they had left the earth and were soaring through a blaze of red, yellow and blue lights. Home, she breathed, home, and she smiled to herself.

When Richard Mayne opened his eyes at last the morning was almost over. The night had passed like an epic dream culminating with Harumi's farewell kiss in the early morning. Could anything so perfect, he asked himself, ever be reconciled with the daylight mind of the human, the reality of things to be done, meaningless timetables to follow. He nuzzled his face into the impression on Harumi's side of the pillow and breathed her name. If it were afterall only a dream he had no need of the actual world.

Wands of sunlight lay on the tatami and over the turmoil of clothes and bedding on the floor. From near and far the song of the city filtered like dust into the room. This morning the city did not jar Mayne's mind, nor did the cries of the baby upstairs. He watched for a moment the union of sun and tatami. Then he got up, yawning and stretching, and went into the bathroom.

In the kitchen he poured fruit juice and toyed with the compulsion to call Harumi at her office. They would not meet again till the following afternoon, and that was decades away. He needed a link with her presence, the certainty of her voice. The telephone was only a step away. He picked up the handpiece and began to dial. No, he must wait. He replaced the receiver. He was not a child. Must wait till Hachiko and the rush of her body toward him.

Turning away Mayne caught sight of the typewriter. It stared up at him, etched in neglect. He shrugged his shoulders and looked away. It would be useless, he thought, to try now. The columns of words stacked in his brain would not reach the page. Instead, her image would imprint itself and lie like a splendid shield between

127

inspiration and outlet. Excuses, he chided forlornly, always miserable, beautiful excuses you bone lazy man. And he moved away.

A dark blue kimono flecked with white passed briskly by the window. The doorbell sounded. Mayne opened the door to the bright, all-seeing eyes of his landlady, Kimura-san. "Good morning," she began in her richly aloof voice, "a beautiful day indeed. Are you well?"

From long-standing custom Mayne responded in kind. On Wednesdays and chance meetings they had passed much time together. He guessed that the file on him in Kimura's head was fatter than the one at Immigration Headquarters. When the preliminaries had been brought to a satisfactory conclusion he said, "Well, can I help you?"

She smiled her most aristocratic landlady smile and shot a professional glance into the interior of the apartment. "I have come on a matter of bad news," she murmured. "It happened only a few hours ago. Michiko is gone."

Mayne felt the sweat squeezing inside the waistband of his pants. "Gone? I don't quite understand. I saw Michiko leaving for work yesterday evening. All seemed well with her then."

"She is dead," Kimura said. "Did you not smell the gas? She died in her bath early this morning."

Why could he not express shock, dismay, disbelief, the normal responses in the aftermath of sudden death? Because, he said to himself, with Michiko there is neither shock nor surprise. This moment in shadow travelled always close to her. "I am sorry to hear this news," he said, "I was completely unaware of it."

Kimura glanced down at the uncollected tray on the flagstones. "You did not hear two hours ago the ambulance, the police car? But then of course you are often busy teaching and so on. Sleep must come late and heavy." She smiled delicately into his eyes.

"How did it happen? Was it without pain?"

"The gas was flowing. A bathtowel was stuffed into the

safety vent. When I saw her she was sitting in the bath. There was a half full bottle of brandy on the bathroom floor. There was no suffering in her face."

In the alley beside Michiko's door Mayne caught a glimpse of Camus's yellow shape. "What can I say?" he said. "She was just over there. I saw her every day. She is gone and I had no chance of knowing her. It is too late now for words." He was suddenly conscious of loss and the burden of his own inadequacy. He needed solitude and the drying breath of the fan. "Have the police completed their enquiries? I mean, are they satisfied that everything was in order?"

"Well, not exactly. There were bruises on her arms and legs." She lowered her voice. "But frankly speaking, that sort of thing was only a hazard of her occupation. The police said they might come back and ask further questions but I think they are too busy for the death of a bar hostess." She smiled graciously and seemed about to turn away then added, "By the way, a new tenant will be taking over Michiko's apartment in a few days. Coincidentally she is also named Michiko. She works in a bar in Shinjuku."

Mayne went inside, stripped off his clothes and stood in front of the fan. As the fevered draughts dried the sweat from his skin and hair he looked over at Michiko's blue door and beyond to the glinting glass and pink concrete of the Rising Sun Plaza. Michiko still unknown at the bottom of the stack. What purpose now the journey that had brought her from the little village, the little village that he could see so clearly in his mind's eye. Tonight the lights would burn brightly again. The blue door would not slam.

Camus appeared framed in the window, perched on a rung of the iron staircase. There was only one interpretation in the yellow eyes and peremptory yowls. Mayne poured milk into a saucer, took it outside and laid it on the flagstones. Returning he watched through the window the lap lapping tongue and weary eyes. There was something in the image of Camus that always strengthened him. When the milk was gone the yellow eyes looked up in brief acknowledgement of Mayne. Then, as if there was some pressing engagement to attend, the cat moved swiftly off past Michiko's door and disappeared into the alley.

"Who are you?" Noguchi said, smiling at the new image in the cubicle mirrors. "Did you say your name was Watanabe. Suzuki, Tamaka? Well, from now on any name will do. Just pluck one from the sky and stick it on like a label as the mood takes you. How do you do, I am Watanabe of no fixed abode, just passing through . . ."

With increasing relish, wonder almost, Noguchi studied the sparkling three dimensional self. And so old Noguchi is gone, you say. Well never mind, here is a stout fellow to step into his boots. He knew the old Noguchi well and had been awaiting this moment for a lifetime. See how brightly the mirrors reflect his eyes. He is like a child in his first planetarium.

Under the red T-shirt the round belly stood out like a cooking pot but time would soon take the surplus away along with the tightness in the black jeans. And in the early days when the stout leather tramping boots pinched there was a pair of comfortable sandals in the pack to change into. Noguchi put back his shoulders and drew in his stomach. No, the switch was complete. Not even that old businessman Noguchi would know him now.

From a hook on the wall he took down his businessman's clothes and with his shoes bundled them into his empty breifcase. Beside the briefcase his new well-filled mountaineer's pack stood. How ludicrous they look side by side, he thought, how disparate the functions. He picked up his things, passed through the curtain and went to the sales desk.

While the sales clerk totted up figures Noguchi took a pair of sunglasses from his jeans, polished them and put them on. When the transaction was completed he walked from the shop with the pack on his back and the wrapped

130

briefcase under his arm. A few steps down the street he found a cluster of garbage cans waiting for collection. As if it was the most natural thing in the world to do he put the wrapped briefcase on top of the pile and with a silent "Goodbye Noguchi, good luck" he moved on.

The pace and character of the Shinjuku streets in daytime was brisker than the nights. It was a weekday and the people, though fewer, were bustling with things to do. Noguchi, pack heavy, hunched like a crab, bumped here and there a back or shoulder. No one seemed to mind or even see him. That's Shinjuku, he thought chuckling to himself, you could step out of a spaceship and walk down the street with three heads and six arms and no one would pay too much attention.

Passing the cafe, camera shops, slot machine parlours and bars Noguchi was gripped with a rising exhilaration. For the first time in his life there was no schedule, no compulsion to begin this or return needlessly to that, no clock to fear, no button to press or answer, no timetable. He knew only vaguely where he was going and it did not matter when he got there. Universal time was on his side now.

He took a flight of steps into the underground and followed a long humid tunnel into the lobby of Shinjuku station. As he was about to dump his pack and buy his ticket a salary man, hurrying head down, barged into him. As the man was about to raise his head and apologise Noguchi recognised him as a junior in his company's head office. But there was no sign of recognition in the young man's eyes. From now, he thought as he went to the ticket window, it will be like another country, each day something new to explore and nothing to bring back the alien past.

A train stood waiting at the platform not yet cleared for boarding. Opposite the unreserved carriages long lines of people waited. There were groups of chattering students sitting on rucksacks, middle-aged farm ladies with empty produce packs, mothers and little children and day labourers. Noguchi stood a little back from one of the

131

queues and lowered his pack. He took out a handkerchief and mopped the sweat from his face. Seeing his bare wrist it dawned on him that his watch too had gone into the briefcase. He was still standing back mopping his face when the carriage doors sprang open and the rush to board began.

Harumi was so mesmerised by the piece of note paper she was pretending to read that she was afraid of falling into some kind of euphoric coma. Not one word had registered. Instead the white page on her desk had become a window into the world of last night, with she and Mayne lying together and the music playing. Through the white window she could see him, touch him, feel the exquisite warmth of his body. "I love you," he had said on parting, and she had replied in English and thought of it in Japanese over and over since.

Through the notepaper she was vaguely conscious of a name being called. The sound swelled, grew more insistent. "Harumi," she heard at last, "telephone." She looked up blushing. Her section chief was holding out the receiver and gazing at her as if she were a stranger who had just come to the office on an errand.

Through the muted rhythm of her surroundings she felt other curious eyes. She lowered her head and brought the receiver like a shield to her face. "This is your uncle Hiroshi," the impassive voice began. "I am afraid there is bad news."

"Is it mother? Is she . . .?" In the midst of the panicked questions in her mind she was surprised at her calm tone of voice. "Please tell me what has happened."

"She has been taken seriously ill. You must come home immediately. A train leaves from Ueno station in an hour. Just come as you are."

The sequence of events from the time Harumi put the receiver down until she climbed aboard the train at Ueno station passed with dream-like unreality. Her section chief had shown genuine practised concern and her colleagues

132

were warm in their commiseration. On the train to Ueno station it had come to her suddenly that she was going home on a work day and without belongings. But she managed the business of changing trains in the maze of Ueno station and the purchase of a ticket. She was even lucky enough to find a spare seat in a reserved carriage.

Now she sat in a comfortable seat with no one beside her and two chatting salary men opposite. The train was moving from the outskirts of Tokyo into the countryside. Rice fields were beginning to appear in the spaces between towns and the lizard backed ranges were taking shape. As the landscape of past journeys painted itself again for her Harumi thought, I did not telephone Richard and I won't be back in time for our meeting at Hachiko tomorrow. Never mind, I'll call him from home as soon as I know about mother.

The two salary men were simmering with enthusiasm over the prospects of their trip. Their destination was a pump factory in a Fukushima city where they were to discuss the installation of a micro-computer system. The destiny of the earth it seemed was dependent on their technology and initiative. Each sipped a can of chilled Asahi beer while they eyed each other and discussed the magnitude of their plan. Unobtrusively Harumi began to study the salary men. The shock was beginning to thaw and there were hours yet before she would be home.

The accumulation of intimacies within her was crying for revelation. Once Keiko would have received them all, detail by detail, minute. Now there was no Keiko to confide in and she was getting further and further from Richard every minute. If only she could place her narrative between the word symbols of the computer men, use them as terminals for the violent flood of her expression. Why not? To all intents and purposes she was invisible to them anyway.

One man said, "And then of course there is the strong point of the 27.4 per cent reduction in man hours in the first year. That has been fully substantiated by calculation." Harumi surveyed the men as if she was

133

gazing at scarecrows in a distant rice field. Do you know what I've been doing all night, she began silently . . .? Well, I'll tell you. I've been making love . . . "Yes, yes," the other man said, "and that will increase to 36.2 per cent the following year."

I haven't slept a wink, Harumi went on, and now I'm on my way home to see my mother, who may be dying. And while I am thinking of my mother I am also thinking of Richard, my lover. Yes, of course, he is a foreigner. Would you say I was a good obedient daughter of Japan?

The two men raised their beer cans and looked expertly at each other. Point after point was stressed and concluded by their mutually nodding heads. Now and then their glances converged with Harumi's but only fleetingly. Meanwhile the flow of her narrative passed unchecked between their voices.

I could not telephone Richard before I left. There was no time. And now he's far away I'm terrified of losing contact with him. Can you understand what contact, being connected, means? For the first time in my life, all of a sudden, I feel the beginning of real understanding and I'm afraid now, terribly afraid, of being cut off.

They rushed through a way station bedecked with a border of high school girls in long black skirts and white blouses gazing with round mouths and intense faces. Harumi's narrative ran on. Just before sunrise this morning he kissed the blue mark low down on my spine. He said it was in honour of four thousand years continuous civilisation, my civilisation. Then he kissed my bottom and took his time over it. I can still feel his lips there. Can you hear me? Can you believe me? After that he moved his lips to my . . . yes, that place . . . that place you are always talking about in the bars of Ginza. Then as the sun was rising we made love again and for the first time in my life I came with a man. It was wonderful. He laughed when I told him I would not take a bath until we met again.

The destination of the salary men was approaching.

Like anglers on a fishing trip they were making a last check of their tackle, discussing tactics, checking hooks. One said, "The order will be a big one and we are practically assured of it." And the other: "Yes, yes, I have a strong feeling we are in luck this time."

Before you depart, Harumi inserted, consider the case of mother and me. She is ill and, as I intimated, may be dying. But try as I may I cannot see her face or imagine her condition. I can only see the face of Richard my lover. Is that not strange to you, computer men?

Yet when I heard my uncle Hiroshi's voice on the telephone I was so afraid. My mother ill, perhaps dying, my mother. And even now my cousin Kazuyo, the first lady doctor in our town, may be holding my mother's pulse and fighting her own fears. Yes, I was so afraid for mother, for me . . . .

The train was slowing. On either side of the tracks houses and freight yards and factory walls were thickening. The salary men stood up clutching their briefcases, still talking without a glance for Harumi. The girl in the green silk dress, Harumi intoned silently, thank you for turning your terminals so patiently to her story. Soon the two men were jostling out of sight down the aisle.

I must look terribly worn out, Harumi thought as the train moved on again. If mother was well one look would tell her instantly what I had been doing. She put her feet up on the empty seat and shut her eyes. But the brief closure of light only took her back more graphically into the events of last night. She looked out at the rushing green rice fields and lizard backed hills and realised suddenly that she was almost home.

When Harumi stepped down at last on to the familiar platform her uncle was waiting by the carriage door. Thin and sharp as a bamboo stake he was as unchanged as ever. In quick succession the anxious queries leapt at him. "How is mother, when did it happen, is she in hospital?" There was nothing in the sun dried face to guide her. The eyes that from first memory had regarded her with either disinterest or contempt had not mellowed.

As they hurried along the platform Hiroshi said, "Under the circumstances she is as well as can be expected. Your cousin Kazuyo is taking good care of her. But no more questions now. Soon you will see yourself."

By the station a new car stood gleaming like a grey shark fresh from the sea. Harumi was not surprised when her uncle opened its doors and ushered her in. As they sped through the town the usual chat about weather and family was dispensed with. In the silence a deadening fatigue like thick blankets wrapping the mind was growing in Harumi. The town flicked mindlessly by.

Hiroshi was parking the car. "You go in now," he said, "I will follow later." She went in quickly through the garden, pausing in the vestibule to take off her shoes. As she was stepping into slippers Kazuyo emerged from the middle room. She wore her white practitioner's smock and her most disarming smile radiated briefly in her plump professional face. After the brief formality of greetings Kazuyo said in her modulated bedside voice, "Please go in. She is waiting. I will return later."

For a long moment Harumi stood poised on the threshold of the middle room scarcely able to believe her eyes. Her mother sat smiling up at her enthroned, slim and elegant, on a cushion on the tatami. She wore a beautiful pale blue kimono and her unlined face was a picture of radiant health. On the table before her cups were laid out for green tea and her hands seemed poised to serve.

Tears dimmed Harumi's eyes. She moved forward, knelt by her mother and embraced her. "But mother," she murmured at last into the scented neck of the kimono, "I was so anxious for you. I came immediately and now . . . you seem so perfectly well and happy."

After a while her mother released her and they sat apart at the table. Tea was served. Following a brief appraisal her mother said, "You look tired, Harumi. Perhaps you should rest now and we could talk later."

"No," Harumi said, "I came home because I was told

you were ill." Little barbs of doubt and fear were snagging in her weary mind. In body and feeling her mother had never looked more vibrantly alive. "This morning I was busy at work. Why was I called away so urgently, mother?"

"Well," her mother began calmly. "Then let us be direct. Three days ago after certain information was received from Tokyo a family meeting was held in this house. It was decided that the circumstances were such that you should return to your home as soon as possible."

"What circumstances?" Harumi fought to keep her voice calm and to follow the thread of her mother's words. "I was living a normal life in Tokyo. I imagined something terrible had happened here."

The smiling mouth was ill-matched with the accusation in the eyes. "You know perfectly well, Harumi, the real reason for seeking your return. You have a lover, a foreigner." Her voice was cold with anger now. "Was that not a good enough reason for bringing you home?"

Harumi stared at her mother in astonishment. It was unbelievable, too ludicrous, surely, to be anything but a figment of her imagination, but it was happening and moment by moment the chill in her mother's eyes was deepening. "Yes, I do have a lover, a foreigner, but did you get me back here on pretext just to hear that?"

The lovely slender hand was serving green tea. "No member of this family on either side has ever been linked with foreign blood. I did not raise you with such care and send you to university so that our family name could be tainted by a shiftless foreigner."

A needle-like pain had begun in Harumi's temple. Whatever charade her mother was playing she would live it through. At Hachiko tomorrow afternoon she would be again with Richard. "No, you sent me to university so my chances of a good marriage would be enhanced, so my family could match me regardless of my feelings with some peerless young man and we could all live happily ever after." She felt her voice beginning to break. "I am 23 and entirely separate from you now. Can't you see it's

137

all so melodramatic to me, unreal. This is not the era of Edo or even Meiji, it's the final part of the twentieth century."

Kazuyo and Hiroshi entered silently and sat a little apart from the table. Harumi noted the swift exchange of glances, the I'm in control half smile on her mother's lips. The softening voice indicated a change of approach. "I know it sounds severe, Harumi, but quite frankly you look so worn out that I feel anything I say would be bound to upset you at this moment." The eyes of Kazuyo and Hiroshi gave tacit confirmation of this. "You need a good long rest, Harumi, and this is still your home no matter how you feel just now."

"I'm returning to Tokyo on the first train in the morning," Harumi said flatly. "I live there and work there, remember?"

The faces of cousin and uncle had tensed. Her mother leaned forward speaking slowly, emphatically, as to a little child. "No, you are mistaken. You did live there, Harumi. Now you are living here. I need you. This house needs you. The family needs you. All your affairs in Tokyo have been settled."

Harumi could scarcely release the words. "What do you mean, settled? I have a job, an apartment in Tokyo. My life is there."

The delicate hand poured tea and placed the cups conveniently for Kazuyo and Hiroshi. "Excuse me, Harumi, but that was a little in the past." She smiled faintly and shook her head. "Today by telephone your uncle Hiroshi arranged the termination of your lease and the forwarding of your belongings to this house." Hiroshi inclined his head gravely. "He also called your office and tendered your resignation for family reasons. The explanation he gave was completely understood. So you see, Harumi, we all have your well-being so much at heart. You have truly come home to stay. In a week or so with lots of rest and plenty of fresh air this will become clear to you."

"Is that true?" Harumi's voice dropped to a whisper. The room was misting. She had to get away quickly and

138

make contact with Richard.

"As true as you are my only child." The cool fingers briefly embraced Harumi's fingers. "But now you must rest . . . ."

The three faces were upside-down cubist. They would not detain her longer. She made her way across the tatami that expanded everywhere like a superb golden pond and found the stairs. The turned wooden hand rail was as cool and smooth as the touch of her mother's skin.

Upstairs Harumi slid open the screens and entered her room. Everything was prepared, the bed immaculate, a vase of slender blue irises in a corner, her stereo records ready to play, the telephone at arm's reach beside the bed.

She went to the telephone and uplifted the handpiece. The stairs had made breathing difficult but she would manage. Carefully she put the receiver down then drew it close again and listened. It lay remote and lifeless in her hand. As she stood in the silence of the childhood room her eyes picked up a small lacquer bowl beside the telephone. Inside there were delicate slices of Kiwifruit — she could clearly smell the exotic richness — and a minute lacquer fork.

All of a sudden everything was incredibly, fantastically funny. Harumi began to giggle. The giggles spilled into laughter and she began to laugh and laugh and laugh. She collapsed on the bed laughing and shaking and rolling from side to side. She felt she could go on laughing for ever and ever but somehow somewhere plump arms came around her and a little dart pricked her and the room began to grow darker and darker . . . .

"It is good you came to me," Kato said. "It is the Japanese way. I can understand your situation. Now is the time when you need the absolute attention of another person." He gave a mock superior smile. "For tonight, all night long, I will listen to your voice, like my English teacher once used to listen to me."

"It's like one of those nightmares that go on and on," Mayne said. "Every moment you imagine you'll wake up and find the ordinary world . . . but I'll try to make what happened as clear as possible for you." They were lying in their underpants in a cleared space on the mutilated wasteland of tatami in Kato's room. Books spilled from the unmade bed and lay in heaps around the walls. Unwashed pots and empty noodle packets littered the sink bench in the tiny alcove.

Kato selected a can of beer from the pack Mayne had brought, gave it to Mayne and took one for himself. "You look so hot," he said. "I'm sorry my room is not more comfortable, but if I paid the electricity charges for a fan I would not be able to buy my instant noodles. Never mind, just try to be relaxed and tell me slowly what happened." He lit a cigarette.

"Well," Mayne said, "I was telling you about Michiko's death. I guess that's where it all began. I thought of her alone in the bath like that and the two of us, Harumi and me, on the other hand, just coming into life. All day I wanted to call Harumi just for the reassurance of her voice but we had promised not to contact each other before our meeting at Hachiko this afternoon." Mayne fixed his eyes on a cigarette burn on the tatami and tried to keep the mounting emotion from his voice.

"Last night I thought the lessons would never end. The students sat like donkeys. I could think only of Hachiko and Harumi coming toward me. My voice seemed to have lost contact with its language. The students stared at me. Can you imagine how slowly the clock ticked?"

"Yes, I know well," Kato said as he stubbed out his cigarette in an overflowing saucer. "At the end of every month while I wait for my allowance each day is like a long lonely year. But please go on."

"At last I got to bed and somehow drifted into sleep. When I awoke this morning I felt better. Today was the day of Hachiko. Do I sound like a crazy foreigner to be so obsessed by a meeting at Hachiko? Can we ever comprehend the inner forces that drive us at times to act like puppets and little children?"

Kato shook his head. "Mostly we like to imagine we are in control," he murmured.

"At noon I set off for Shibuya. I was four and a half hours early but I couldn't stand being shut up in the apartment any longer. It was like walking a treadmill in a Turkish bath. By the time I got to Shibuya station I was in a lather of sweat. I sat in that coffee bar by the station, you know the one, cooling down with iced orange and watching the crowd around the fountain and by the dog. I saw joy lighting the faces as each couple met. Soon I would be sharing that joy . . . with Harumi."

In the smoky half light their eyes met and held for a moment. "As you know," Kato said, "I also have some experience of Hachiko. I understand clearly."

"After a while I took a walk in the streets of Shibuya. Sort of lost myself among the people." As he attended the rise and fall of his voice Mayne was seeing again sharp and clear each detail of the afternoon. "Then I went to Seibu department store and wandered around in there for a while. I soon got tired of looking at things as if they meant something to me, so I left and headed straight for Hachiko. In the back of my mind all the time I guess I didn't want to be too far away from that place.

"I was about an hour early but I kept saying to myself, you never know, she might be early too. I didn't mind standing there in the heat with all the traffic noise and people. Just watching the faces of Hachiko is the most intriguing form of entertainment I know. I played my usual game trying to figure out who was waiting and who was simply watching the waiting."

Kato handed over a can of beer and lit a cigarette. "Sometimes when I pass there," he said, "I stand and watch. It's fascinating."

"Five minutes before Harumi was due my heart began to thump as if it was anxious to escape from my body. I wondered what she was wearing. Perhaps it would be the same green silk dress she wore the other day and was also wearing when we first met. I was uncertain of the direction from which she would be coming so I walked around the fountain on the fringe of the crowd. I did everything to make sure she could not possibly miss me. Does that sound crazy too?"

141

"No, of course not," Kato said, "I've done it myself many times."

"At four thirty exactly a girl in a green dress emerged from the crowd in the street and came hurrying toward me. I was about to rush forward when I realised it was not Harumi. In the next five minutes or so I saw many Harumis in the distance but not my Harumi. From then I just kept on waiting, thinking of all kinds of reasons why she would turn up in the end — a misunderstanding over the meeting time, being kept late at the office? I stayed like that for three hours saying to myself every few moments, I'll go now, but not being able to move an inch from that place by the fountain and the dog."

Mayne observed Kato's extra agitated cigarette hand. "Yes, I know what you would like to say — that I knew all the time she would not turn up, and I did have that kind of premonition too, probably since the day before yesterday. I had to think she would come. I would rather have died than face the alternatives.

"Fortunately I had my notebook with me. I went into the station and called her office. It was after 7.30 by then but I was lucky enough to contact her section chief who was working late. He was courteous, as you may imagine, but within his voice there was a locked vault. Harumi had resigned suddenly from the company, he told me, and he did not know her whereabouts. He could give me only her apartment telephone number, which of course I already had.

"It was useless to ask further questions. When a foreigner is shut out there's no way of getting back in again. The exclusion is also quite contagious. If I approached anyone at the bank they would give me the identical information the section chief had already passed on. Before I left the station I called Harumi's apartment number. Of course there was no answer.

"I took a taxi and went in search of Harumi's apartment house. I knew it was not far from Shibuya. After a lot of running around I finally managed to locate the landlady. She opened the door a crack and looked at me without the usual consternation that's present when a

142

foreigner unexpectedly appears. While she greeted me her voice gave little away but her eyes were two doors, shut and barred. Yes, Harumi had left suddenly and she had no idea where she had gone. A forwarding agent had come and collected all her belongings. If it would help she could give me Harumi's telephone number at the bank . . . that was all she knew."

Mayne paused to drink some beer and mop his sweating face. "So then you came here," Kato said. "The trail had come to an end."

"Yes, it was almost dark. I walked all the way. If I'd just heard of Harumi's death I could not have felt more lonely or cut off from the life around me. But every step I took I knew she was alive and in some way trying to make contact with me. I didn't know where I was going. I just seemed to find myself by your door. You know the ways of your country. Tell me what you think of this."

Kato shook his head. "It's difficult to say. She may be with her family." He paused then murmured, "It sounds severe but no matter where she may be now I think you will not see her again. It is better that you accept this now. She is gone but in your heart she will always be your lover."

And we will all live happily ever after, Mayne thought, close to weeping. The pinpoint of his mind that remained in control had anticipated Kato's thought, but to have it expressed aloud, will not see, will not see, was intolerable. "Then there's no way out," Mayne said almost in a whisper. "It's just beginning to hit me now."

"Time is the way out," Kato said, "and for you there is another way."

Mayne put down his beer can and lay back on the tatami. "What do you mean?"

A trace of the old sneer returned to twist Kato's lips. His voice climbed incongruously higher. "Have you forgotten what you told me so many times? You said when deep torment enters the mind don't try to escape. Instead, you told me, no matter how frightening it may be at times, pass through the eye of the experience, turn the torment into words, write it all down. As the words fill the page the mind will empty itself of pain." Kato recited this carefully as if reading it from a book.

Mayne put his hands over his eyes, more to shut out light than stop the tears. Vaguely he felt Kato's warmth drawing closer, the roughly tender fingers stroking his forehead. His chest began to heave. "It's good," Kato whispered. "It's good. Let it all go now . . . ."

To the crunching rhythm of his boots on the road Noguchi felt the village falling away behind him. It was the last village on the old branch line and the last cluster of people between himself and the mountains. He had taken a bowl of noodles in a little place that was more like a farm kitchen than a cafe and chatted with the lady about the weather and crops, listening to the lady's unhurried dialect and feeling the unfolding of space and calm. He was delighted that his lack of planning had bought him such a remote beginning. The end of the line, he had mused, what a perfect place to begin.

He had just passed a little girl eating an icecream who had stopped to introduce herself with laughing, candid eyes, and before that an ancient couple had passed heading for the village, the man in a heavy dark suit and the woman in formal kimono holding a parasol aloft. They greeted him like an old friend and then went tottering on their way. Off to a wedding, Noguchi thought. Another beginning, another ending . . . .

At the end of the road many hours away an inn was waiting in the foothills. It will be up there, Noguchi thought, raising his eyes, there where the green turns to grey blue, under the purple rim of the mountains. But it was only a game, an imagined point of guidance. He could not foretell the twist and turn of the road. He had only to follow its course.

The sun was high. There was not a breath of wind. As the village faded the sounds of the countryside began to harmonize. Noguchi became more and more conscious of the massed chanting of the locusts and the half

144

remembered singing of birds. In the free moments of childhood he would lie in the long grass facing the sky and let the music of the seasons into his mind. Soon the loneness of the little boy who thought and dreamed too much for his own good was lost in the rapturous trilling of a bird or the whirring wings of a dragonfly.

Now it seemed as Noguchi walked on into the fresh singing world that a great wall had been built around all that lay behind him. Once there was a businessman . . . what is a businessman? . . . whose head was filled with dreams. Slowly, because of the detachment of his poet's eye and mind (he could never say he was a poet) from the everyday business of life around him he became invisible. When he at last disappeared altogether those who had known him or thought they had known him were nagged by doubts of his ever having existed at all. He was gone but the wall stood thick and high without a crack or needlepoint of light.

Whatever happened to Noguchi? He looked . . . well, never mind, you remember. They say at Shinjuku station in rush hour one day his head exploded into a million tiny pieces, too minute to trace. There was nothing left but his briefcase, and that only contained a watch, a pair of shoes and a businessman's uniform. Of course I did not know him myself, I only heard about him vaguely here and there . . . . You can never get to know a Noguchi, that is understood. A strange case . . . .

Back from the road half hidden in a grove of giant bamboo and birch an old temple stood. While Noguchi paused to wipe his dripping face he surveyed the temple. The sagging earth-brown walls were almost obscured by foliage and the slate grey roof seemed to be softening into sky and leaf. By divine neglect the temple appeared to be settling back into the earth. Mayne, on approaching the scene, would ask in his foreigner's way, "Is it Kamamura or early Edo . . .? I mean, how old is the temple?"

Noguchi hoisted his pack and moved on. How old indeed. As old as the hills up there and the purple mountains beyond, as old as Basho, older than the sun, as old as yesterday and tomorrow, as old as the song of the locust, as old as now . . . . How old is the temple indeed! With steps linked with the slow swaying of the pack Noguchi walked steadily on up the climbing road.

In the frame of the open window Camus appeared on the iron staircase. At first Mayne thought the cat was alone but the undulations of the yellow fur and the rising tortured cries soon showed otherwise. The mouth was bent on a scrawny black neck and the yellow eyes blazed straight in the window at Mayne. Look at me, man, in my prime, envy me, man, the eyes told Mayne.

Mayne grinned and felt the grin broadening. It was the first time it seemed he had smiled for an age. "I don't envy you, Camus," he said. "I just don't know how you can burn up so much energy in this heat." He turned away and caught the fresh white page in the typewriter staring up at him.

The last few days had passed in a confusion of intent and lethargy. Every morning when he had eaten and bathed he sat at the typewriter ready to begin. The assembled text, so nurtured and processed in the mind, cried only for release. He hunched over the machine, tense, expectant. Now it will find its way to the page . . . I know it will. An hour, two hours later, he would leave the empty page and begin to pace the room. Each barren morning was an exact replica of the last.

The shrieking, moaning cats had begun to drown the whining fan. Suddenly like a giant firecracker going off Michiko's door slammed. The cats, to Mayne's wondering eye, seemed to leap straight up in separate arcs into the pale blue sky. A figure stood in front of the blue door jingling a jingle-bell keyring. Mayne stood at the window, his nostrils quivering. The new Michiko, he mused, freshly risen from the bath.

She was draped in a long white blouse and sleek black skirt. Her shoes were whispers of black suede. In the strong sunlight her hair shone like lacquered ebony. As if she had sensed the eyes all the while she turned suddenly and looked directly at Mayne. In the broad, smooth,

146

northern Honshu face the eyes flashed. Well you never know what to expect in a big city — even a hairy foreigner in broad daylight and in the most unlikely of places. For a moment she bent and fumbled with her purse and shopping bag.

Mayne stood fascinated, unable to leave the window. Younger, a little slimmer, the bright new Michiko was about to be launched. The same fiery spirit he recalled from a few summers earlier frisking, to meet the world. "Go to it, Michiko," he said under his breath. "Better luck this time."

As if about to walk on to a stage Michiko tossed her head, drew in her buttocks and thrust forward her breasts. Then she started across the courtyard, sending the bath-fresh wafts of perfume rippling through Mayne's window. He watched until her head bobbed out of sight below the level of the steps.

Upstairs the baby was crying, too hot and fretful to be soothed any more by the mother's crooning. Not far away between the hum and burp of traffic and the intermittent screeching of trains a boy was whistling a traditional folk song. Mayne sat down at the typewriter and arched his fingers above the keys. A face began to appear on the snow white paper. Beginning words came haltingly into his mind.

The keys tapped uncertainly at first. Overhead the baby's crying was falling to a whimper. The face grew clearer, the face of a woman, lips forming words. Above, the mother's feet squeaked the tatami. The first line had crossed the page clear and black. The keys tapped faster.

Mayne felt the exhiliration in his temples and fingers. In the alley water was splashing. The mounting tempo of words triggered more lines across the page. The baby's whimperings were fading into sleep. Morning was melting into noon. Mayne drew out the first page and quickly rolled another into place.

147

"PET SHOP"
REVIEWS

"One word describes Ian Middleton's first novel – excellent." Auckland Star, 12.8.81

"It's unusual to find a New Zealand novel so rich in passion as "Pet Shop." Evening Standard, 24.7.81

"Ian Middleton's debut as a novelist is deserving of acclamation." New Zealand Woman's Weekly, 24.8.81

"'Pet Shop' is valuable both as a record of an earlier but not so distant New Zealand, and as a fictional creation." Nelson Evening Mail, 18.3.80